Perfect Run as No. 1

BRIAN LESTER

Aquitaine Ltd
Phoenix, Arizona

Cover design by JD Smith Designs

Library of Congress Control Number: 2017952457

ISBN-13: 978-0-9980858-3-8
ISBN-10: 0-9980858-3-9

www.aquitaineltd.com

DEDICATION

For the University of Findlay men's basketball team,
the Oilers, who came to embrace the pressure rather
than let it serve as a burden.

PROLOGUE

Only the sound of my fingertips rapidly tapping the keyboard of my laptop as I sat on press row sliced through the silence of the Grand Valley State Fieldhouse in Allendale, Mich., on the night of March 18, 2008.

I was under the pressure of deadline for The Courier, a daily newspaper in Findlay, Ohio, and in the midst of writing my game story on the gut-wrenching end to an NCAA Division II championship quest for the University of Findlay men's basketball team. On a night when it seemed the Oilers were destined for glory, destined to return to the Elite Eight for the first time since 2005, destiny was not on their side. Everything that could have gone wrong that night did for Findlay in a Sweet 16 showdown against Grand Valley State, a bitter but respected rival in the Great Lakes Intercollegiate Athletic Conference. The Lakers entered the game at 35-0 and co-owners of the No. 1 ranking in the nation with Winona State out of Minnesota. Twice

1

during the season Grand Valley humbled Findlay, both times in Allendale, including in December when it clobbered the Oilers 82-60.

The second time was in the championship game of the GLIAC tournament, 10 days before their battle in the NCAA tournament. Findlay played hard but its rally attempt fell short in a 73-67 loss, adding more fuel onto the fire of one of the most physical and heated rivalries in a conference featuring schools in Ohio and Michigan.

The latest encounter on a Tuesday night in mid-March was supposed to be different in an arena that, in past games, had been a house of horrors for Findlay. Winning here was rare, not just for Findlay, but for any team. Still, the Oilers went into the game optimistic and eager for revenge. Instead, the game played out like a nightmare.

Findlay was beaten and bruised by the Lakers, who dominated over the course of 40 minutes of basketball and, finally, lost 75-58 in front of a frenzied, sold-out crowd. A day earlier, head coach Ron Niekamp, who retired in 2011 without ever having a losing campaign in his 27 seasons with the Oilers, was well aware his team would have its hands full against the Lakers, who were gunning for a second consecutive trip to the Elite Eight.

"They have great athletes and are a very deep team," Niekamp said of the Lakers after the Oilers bounced Gannon University from the regional tournament, with an 88-82 win in the semifinal round on Sunday night. "They have made us look pretty ordinary the first two times we played them. We need to search for answers and come up with a good game plan."

Niekamp and his staff were excellent when it came to preparing the Oilers for a game, and he and his assistant coaches stuck around after the game against Gannon to scout the Lakers in their regional semifinal battle with Northern Kentucky. In this instance, the preparation was little help against a Lakers team that owned the night, setting the Oilers' game plan on fire with a stellar shooting performance and a sensational effort on defense.

The blue-clad crowd roared every time one of the eleven 3-pointers the Lakers hit ripped through the net. The band played its music at a deafening level every time the Oilers had to burn a timeout to try to figure out a way to slow down the Lakers, who seemed to have as much momentum as a train speeding down a track at 200 miles an hour.

Shots wouldn't fall with any sort of consistency and the Oilers struggled to string together defensive stops against a Lakers team with a golden shooting touch. That golden touch was most evident in Jason Jamerson and Pete Trammell, the most dangerous outside shooters in the Lakers' talented lineup. Jamerson and Trammell knocked down four 3-pointers apiece to punctuate their 17-point efforts. As Jim Heller, my friend and the voice of the Oilers that season, would later tell me, the Secret Service couldn't have guarded Jamerson and Trammell that night.

The Lakers shot 47.8 percent from the field and hit eleven of their seventeen attempts from beyond the arc. They led 42-25 at halftime and went 15-of-18 from the free-throw line in the second half to kick the final piles of dirt onto the Oilers' grave.

"I thought our strong start was big for us," Grand

Valley head coach Ric Wesley said in a post-game interview. "We shot the ball extremely well, and we did a lot of good things on defense to make it difficult for them to come back."

It seemed no matter how hard the Oilers worked to scratch and claw their way back into the game, they stayed two steps behind the Lakers, shooting only 37.1 percent from the floor, a surprising statistic for a team that came in as one of the best shooting teams in the nation at 51.5 percent. Josh Bostic, the undisputed team leader who was named an All-American at the end of the season, scored 19 points. Starting point guard Marcus Parker poured in 15 points, and Morgan Lewis, Bostic's best friend and one of the most athletic players on the team, scored 10 points. No one else scored more than six. The balanced attack Findlay counted on so often during a 28-5 season was nonexistent, mainly because of how well and how hard the Lakers played on defense.

When the clock mercifully hit zero and the Lakers kicked off their celebration, hoisting the regional championship trophy as their fans cheered, the last thing the Oilers wanted to do was stick around to watch the thrill of the moment unfold for Grand Valley. Players wore looks of disappointment and pulled their sweat-soaked jerseys over their heads to avoid watching the Lakers bask in the glory of a Sweet 16 victory. Known for its football success, Grand Valley won four national titles in a five-year span during the decade, its win over the Oilers added to its growing basketball reputation.

The loss cut deep enough that Findlay had a hard time accepting the regional runner-up trophy, and once it did, the players slowly walked to the locker room, shaking their heads in disbelief, while trying to shake off the pain that consumed them. The Oilers spent a lot of time in the locker room after the loss. I could only begin to imagine the pain that enveloped the team as the players reflected on the most disappointing night of their season and, quite frankly, the darkest hour in program history. When they did emerge, they didn't waste time with excuses.

"They were the better team tonight," Bostic said. "We didn't play our best game."

The game turned in the first half, the Oilers falling behind by nearly 20 points. That kind of deficit on the road, especially against the Lakers, was not a great situation to be in.

"Grand Valley played a superb first half," Niekamp said after the game. "We did a good job on All-American center, Callistus Eziukwu, 8 points, but only 2 in the first half, but their other guys like Jamerson and Trammell stepped up and hit some big 3-pointers. It made it difficult for us to make the game more competitive."

I'm not sure anyone ever had the feeling the game was competitive and, as midnight approached; I was trying to sum up the horrible ending to an otherwise remarkable season.

One of the best teams in the country all year, the Oilers had the talent to contend for a title, but against the Lakers, they didn't play unable to their potential. They made too many mistakes and never got into a rhythm, although a lot of credit goes to the Lakers for making that happen.

As I prepared to wrap up my game story, I thought about the potential the Oilers had going into the 2008-09 campaign. Findlay had all five starters coming back and only Tyler Niekamp wasn't returning. Niekamp was a role player who always gave everything he had when he played. Tears were in his eyes as he talked about the end of his career.

"It hurts but this experience at Findlay is probably one of the best of my life," said Niekamp, who was Ron's nephew and would stay on as a grad assistant coach the following season. "It's something I will never forget."

The pain of the Sweet 16 loss was something the Oilers would not soon forget. It simmered on their minds in the offseason and served as motivation for the 2008-09 season ahead.

"It hurt a lot but the loss will motivate us for next season," Bostic agreed. "We still have one more year and that makes us hungry for success. But we won't take anything for granted. We have a lot of work to do."

Lewis echoed those thoughts. He knew there was a long road ahead for the Oilers but the feeling of what could be accomplished during the 2008-09 season was enough to help ease the pain.

"It was a bittersweet feeling for the team," Lewis said, in an interview five years after the championship. "We were obviously upset after being eliminated, but I think the excitement and enthusiasm for the next season was the dominant emotion. We knew that senior season, something special was going to happen. I think we all knew that, the players, the coaches, the community. Everyone knew."

For the moment, however, the sting of the loss burned, especially for Bostic and Lewis, who were determined to never forget the pain as they prepared to set the tone for their senior season. The veteran teammates were the brightest stars and the best of friends. They knew each other as well as any two players could. Over their careers they talked about their drive and desire to win a championship, and now they were on the cusp of their final opportunity to help deliver a title to Findlay.

Bostic and Lewis were part of a heralded Findlay recruiting class that arrived on campus in 2005 and would be counted on for leadership and the ability to step up on any given night. Bostic knew what potential the Oilers had, but he also knew it would take a lot of work to make the dream of a championship a reality. Challenges awaited the Oilers on their 2008-09 journey, including personal ones for Bostic and Lewis. Yet, the two had the support of each other and their teammates and were determined to lead Findlay on its title quest.

"We have to work hard to reach our potential," Bostic said. "We'll get better during the offseason and come into next year with a chip on our shoulder."

The potential Bostic mentioned was the one glimmer of hope this team could hang onto. No one knew it at the time but the Oilers were only months away from embarking on the journey of a lifetime. Out of the ashes of the devastating loss, a team for the ages would rise up and put together one of the greatest seasons in small-college basketball history.

1 BEING NO. 1

When the preseason Division II basketball poll was released on a sun-splashed morning in early October, there was no surprise at the top. Findlay, with five seniors among the returnees, was No. 1, marking the first time in program history it would start the season as the top team in the country. Bostic was tabbed as the preseason National Player of the Year.

So often, the seductive hype of the preseason is never met when the games count, making it rare for the team that begins the season at No. 1 to end the season with the championship, let alone run the table Entering the 2008-09 season, only three Division II teams had ever gone unbeaten enroute to a national championship, the last being Fort Hays State in Kansas in 1996. Only two teams in Division II could make the claim that they had gone wire-to-wire as the No. 1 team in the land. Cal State Bakersfield was the last to do it in 1993, winning the first of back-to-back championships.

Coach Niekamp was in Atlanta watching his

youngest daughter, Allie, play volleyball for Georgia Tech the day the poll was released and so I wasn't able to get up with Niekamp to talk to him about his team's place in the national spotlight but I did talk with Charlie Ernst, his long-time assistant who became the head coach of the Oilers in 2011 when Niekamp retired. Ernst had been with Niekamp for nearly twenty years as a coach and, prior to coaching, he played for Niekamp at Findlay. Ernst had opportunities to go to bigger schools to coach but his loyalty to the program was undeniable. I reached Ernst by phone in the evening and we talked about what the No. 1 ranking meant to the program. The Oilers had not been the top-ranked team in the country since the 2004-05 season, when they finished the regular season at No. 1 and played in the Elite Eight for the first time. The only other time the Oilers had been the top-ranked team was in February of 2005. They were traveling home from Pennsylvania after a two-game road swing against Gannon and Mercyhurst, and one of the assistant coaches learned by phone that the No. 1 team at the time had lost, which meant the No. 2 Oilers were about to rise to No. 1 in the next poll. I was with the team on that trip and remember the excitement of the players when they heard the news. In the 2005 Elite Eight, the Oilers lost 75-66 to Lynn University from Florida in the national quarterfinals at North Dakota's Ralph Englestad Arena. The profile of the Findlay basketball program rose significantly because of the appearance and the success of the season helped bring in the players who would make up the senior class of the 2008-09 team. For Ernst, the lofty preseason ranking was the ultimate sign of respect for a program rich in basketball tradition.

"It's flattering and shows people have respect for our program," Ernst said. "When we first joined Division II, no one thought we would be in this position a decade later. It goes to show that hard work and having good players and coaches can lead to success."

All five starters were returning for the Oilers, who were coming off their seventh consecutive 20-win season and made their seventh consecutive appearance in the NCAA tournament. Past success and preseason accolades weren't a topic of discussion for the team, during the early weeks of practice.

"The thing Ron and I have been preaching to the players is we haven't won anything yet," Ernst said in the interview. "We didn't win the GLIAC South last year, we didn't win the conference tournament last year and we didn't win a national championship last year. We need to work hard and continue to improve throughout the year. If we do that, we have a chance to accomplish something special."

As tempting as it was for the Oilers to look ahead, it wasn't an option.

"We aren't going to look at the big picture right now," Ernst said. "If we stay focused, everything else will take care of itself."

2 BASKETBALL AND FRIENDSHIP

Bostic and Lewis didn't know each other prior to coming to Findlay, both hailing from different cities in Ohio. Bostic, who told me he once considered playing college football, was from Columbus while Lewis hailed from Painesville, a city outside of Cleveland. The one thing they had in common, though, was unbelievable basketball talent.

"I didn't know Josh at all coming into Findlay and, most likely, he had never heard of me," Lewis said, as he recalled the early days of his collegiate hoops career.

Interestingly enough, even though they were teammates with unlimited potential it wasn't enough to forge the friendship that would be instrumental in leading the Oilers to a championship.

"We didn't actually start off on the right foot and got into a fight late one night during our freshman year," Lewis said. "Times have changed and Josh is one of my closest friends. I have a lot of respect for Josh, as a person and for his family."

The respect shared between Bostic and Lewis grew over the course of their four years together. Neither player was a star in their first two seasons, although Bostic started all but two games as a sophomore. Lewis only played in ten games in his second season because he was ineligible most of the year, in part because the health problems his father was dealing with made it difficult to focus on school. It was in their junior seasons the two began to take on more prominent roles, both starting all 33 games, and while their play was pivotal to the success the Oilers enjoyed enroute to the Sweet 16 in 2008, they had their moments where it looked as if it was difficult for them to be on the same page.

"To the outside, it may be looked like Morgan and I clashed on the court in our junior year, but that wasn't it at all," Bostic said, during an interview in the summer of 2014. "We were still working on our roles and working to be leaders. We pushed each other and made each other better players."

Their competitive nature not only made Bostic and Lewis great friends but it made them great players as well. They went at it hard against each other in practice, generating game-like intensity, often to the point where, to an outsider, it looked as if Bostic and Lewis were rivals on opposing teams.

"Sometimes our practices were actually more intense than the games," Bostic said. "We talked trash to each other and played hard. It wasn't competitive in a bad way where we didn't like each other. It was just about having a competitive spirit and playing as hard as we could every day."

Lewis compared the intensity in practice to brothers fighting with each other.

"There were numerous occasions where fights almost broke out," Lewis said. "When we go out and compete against someone every day because we want to get better, it's going to get a little emotional. But it's like brothers fighting in the basement. When it's over, we hug and make up, figuratively speaking."

The competitive fire that burned inside Bostic and Lewis went beyond practices and game day. They often played one-on-one against each other at the campus rec center and, at times, their desire to battle on the court on their own time was sometimes fueled by their video game rivalry.

"I can't even begin to talk about the number of times we got kicked out of the rec center or Croy Gymnasium late on Sunday nights or in the evening during the week for not having scheduled time for the gym," Lewis said. "We would sit at home and play NBA2K or Mortal Kombat on XBox and it would become a winner-loser thing. Then someone would say 'You can't beat me in one-on-one, though,' and we would put the controllers down and head over to the gym to play one-on-one or a game of 21."

The mixture of competitiveness and chemistry was a winning combination, a combination teams simply could not match when Bostic and Lewis were on the floor together, especially during their senior season. They trusted each other with their lives and could count on each other no matter what, something not easily found between two stars. Bostic and Lewis made it work and gave the Oilers every reason to believe they were capable of winning a title.

"It's a major part of our success," Bostic said, before the start of the 2008-09 season. "We've had our ups and downs but we support each other. We always have each other's backs. We have a great friendship, on and off the court. Really, everyone on this team gets along and that is rare. We all want what is best for the team."

Lewis had similar thoughts and said the quest to be champions only strengthened their friendship as they prepared to guide the Oilers through the season ahead.

"The fact that we are so hungry plays a big part in our friendship," Lewis told me, during an interview late in the season. "We have a common goal and that's to win a championship. The easiest way to get there is with each other. On top of playing together the last four years, we are great friends off the court and that makes a big difference.

3 SETTING THE STAGE FOR THE TITLE RUN

The wheels for the national championship season were put in motion long before it ever tipped off. Findlay made the jump to NCAA Division II in 1997, ending its long-standing affiliation with the National Association of Intercollegiate Athletics (NAIA). Yet, the Oilers had to wait five years after the move to be eligible for postseason play; the Oilers couldn't compete in the NCAA tournament during their inaugural season in Division II. When the Oilers became eligible, they capitalized on the opportunity, earning a trip to the 2002 tournament. Only 48 teams made the NCAA tournament that year—the field wasn't expanded to 64 until 2003—and the Oilers entered the tournament with a 22-6 record. Despite being a first-time participant, the Oilers handled the challenge well and made school history with a 70-53 win over Gannon in the opening round at the SportsCenter in Owensboro, KY. The first three rounds of the NCAA tournament are played at the home of the top team in each of the regions, and Kentucky Wesleyan had the luxury of being the host team that season for the Great Lakes Regional. The Purple Panthers were a national power and owners of a record eight Division II national championships. They were also the next opponent for the Oilers, who didn't have much time to savor their first NCAA tournament win in program history.

Kentucky Wesleyan was in the hunt for its first national championship since 1999 but intimidation was not an issue for the Oilers, who shut the hostile crowd out of their minds and gave Kentucky Wesleyan all it could handle, even with the pressure rising late in the game inside the SportsCenter. The Purple Panthers, ranked No. 1 in the nation, were on the ropes against an Oilers team with visions of a monumental upset on its mind. Ultimately, Kentucky Wesleyan prevailed, hanging on for a 94-89 victory. The loss stung but the Oilers didn't come away empty-handed.

"Making that regional and playing Kentucky Wesleyan was the turning point for us," Ernst said during an interview in 2005. "We got an idea of how good we needed to be to get recognition as an elite team. It put our program in the national spotlight."

Staying in the national spotlight was the trick and the route the Oilers would take to remain there was up in the air, as they settled in for the bus ride back to Ohio. Ernst said he and Niekamp talked on that trip about the future of the program and what it would take for Findlay to one day win a national championship. One question helped set the stage for Findlay's championship quest. It centered on how to build a team that could contend for a title. Many of the schools in the Great Lakes Valley Conference, the conference Kentucky Wesleyan was from, built their programs around Division I transfers. Findlay, however, built its program by recruiting high school athletes and developing them over the course of their careers. Both routes had the potential to lead to success. The Oilers had to decide if their way was the right way.

"I will never forget Ron asking if we needed to go out and get Division I transfers in order to compete at the national level," Ernst said during an interview in 2007. "I told him no. I didn't know if it was the right answer, but it was the right thing to say at the time."

The Oilers returned to the NCAA tournament in 2003 and lost again to Kentucky Wesleyan, falling 83-68 to the Purple Panthers after opening the tourney with an 80-76 win over Northern Kentucky. A year later, the Oilers edged Indianapolis 84-83 in overtime in the opening round of the tourney but were taken out by Southern Indiana 75-67 in the second round. It was almost as if a wall was blocking the Oilers from getting to the Sweet 16 and playing for the right to advance to the Elite Eight. Their fortune changed during the 2004-05 season. The Oilers had a team built to be a champion.

"We want to go out there and show people we have a great program," senior guard Matt Metzger said before the start of the 2005 NCAA tournament. "We have a chance to show the region just how good of a team we have."

The Oilers had been making statements all season,

rising to No. 1 in the country in February, and they took a 27-3 record into the NCAA tournament. Their overwhelming success put them in a position to host the regional, and it proved to be a huge advantage for a team that rarely lost at home. Findlay opened the tournament with an 88-73 win over Quincy and then toppled GLIAC rival Wayne State 63-49 in the semifinal round. The Oilers had also beaten Wayne State in the conference tournament, and the two postseason victories over the Warriors made up for a 79-72 loss to Wayne State in Detroit on Valentine's Day. That loss was the last one the Oilers would suffer in the regular season, and the NCAA win over the Warriors catapulted the Oilers into the Sweet 16 for the first time.

Waiting on the opposite side of the matchup was Ferris State, another GLIAC foe. A trip to the Elite Eight in North Dakota was on the line and a sold-out crowd was on hand to witness the historic game. It turned out to be a one-sided affair, the Oilers dominating the Bulldogs from start to finish and rolling to a 94-73 win. Music blared through the gym as the crowd cheered and the players celebrated. Dustin Pfeifer, the point guard for the Oilers, jumped into the arms of Niekamp as he came out of the game with just minutes remaining. The win over Ferris State was easily one of the most thrilling and rewarding moments in the history of a proud Findlay program. So much work had gone into getting to an Elite Eight and, now, regardless of the outcome, the belief had been established the Oilers were capable of competing for a national championship. The trip to North Dakota ended in disappointment, as the Oilers were bounced off the tournament trail by Lynn in a national quarterfinal.

Competing for a title isn't easy and the climb to get back to an Elite Eight for the Oilers was filled with difficult moments. In 2006, when the seniors on the 2008-09 Findlay team were freshmen, the Oilers lost 74-66 in the opening round of the NCAA tournament to Quincy. A year later, the Oilers seemed poised for a championship. They ran the table in the GLIAC and their only loss in the regular season was an 85-82 overtime setback to Tarleton State during a season-opening tournament in Texas.

Findlay earned the right to host the regional for the second time in three seasons and surged past Wisconsin-Parkside 74-60 in the opening round; yet, a cruel twist of fate awaited the Oilers in the next round as their magical season drew to a close with a 60-56 loss to Northern Kentucky. The ending to the Northern Kentucky game is one of the most painful memories in program history. For as long as I live, I will never forget Dorian Bass, a senior, taking a 3-pointer in the closing seconds of regulation against Northern Kentucky. If the shot goes in, the game is tied at 59-59 and overtime is the likely scenario. Instead, the ball and net did not see eye-to-eye. I glanced up at the clock as the shot bounced off the rim and still remember seeing only three-tenths of a second left on the clock. The Norse ended up with the rebound and hit a free throw to seal the deal. Bass scored 18 points that afternoon, leaving everything he had on the floor, which is what you expect from a senior. I felt so bad for Bass and the rest of the team. It was a cruel end to an otherwise remarkable season and the tears in the eyes of those seniors is one of the other lasting images from that day.

The loss to the Lakers in the 2008 Sweet 16 hurt, as well. The thing is, looking back now, those two painful tournament losses served as motivation for the Oilers as they headed into the 2008-09 season. Those seniors, including Bostic, Lewis, Lee Roberts, Tyler Evans, and Aaron Laflin, were determined not to let their final season end with their dream of a title denied and were ready to chase their dream all the way to the finish line.

4 HEARTBREAK FOR BOSTIC

Bostic lived up to every expectation placed on his shoulders during the Oilers' quest for a championship, and on the night of March 17th, he had Findlay on the doorstep of the Elite Eight. Findlay was set to play Bellarmine in the Sweet 16 at Croy Gymnasium, and as focused as Bostic was on rising to the occasion, his mind was also on Javonte Clanton, one of his closest friends and the starting point guard for South Carolina-Aiken. Clanton transferred to Aiken from Blinn Junior College in Texas before the start of the 2008-09 season, and he and Bostic talked all year about the possibility of playing each other in the Elite Eight.

Now, on a mid-March night, the two were on the cusp of making the dream come true. While the Oilers faced off against the Knights for the Midwest Regional crown, Clanton and the Pacers were 678 miles away in Georgia at the Christenberry Fieldhouse, the home of Augusta State and the site of the Southeast Regional championship game. With the way the bracket was set up, the Oilers and Pacers had an opportunity to meet in the national title game. The friendship between Bostic and Clanton went back a decade. They became friends in grade school, spending much of their time together at the Boys and Girls Club in Columbus. They were also teammates on a travel basketball team in grade school. In high school, they were on rival teams in the Ohio Capital Conference and squared off for the league title when Bostic was a senior at Columbus Westland and Clanton was a junior at Reynoldsburg. Being able to play each other in the NCAA tourney was something both players looked forward to and the two talked the day of their respective games, wishing each other luck, and hoping for the best.

"We talked a lot that season about maybe playing against each other in the national tournament. It was exciting thinking about it," Bostic said. "We talked about how things might go. We were really looking forward to making it happen."

Bostic was at his best in the Sweet 16, torching the Knights for 37 points in arguably the greatest performance by a player in Findlay history when you factor in the amount of pressure riding on the moment. His effort was enough to lift the Oilers to an 89-86 overtime win against the Knights, propelling them to a regional title and a spot in the Elite Eight. Clanton, who came into the game against Augusta State as Aiken's third-leading scorer, averaging 11.9 points per game, struggled through a rare off night. He scored only four points as Augusta State rolled past Aiken with an 86-57 victory. The dream of Bostic and Clanton playing each other in the tourney was over, but that news would pale in comparison to what would follow. As Bostic celebrated with his teammates and friends late Tuesday night, Clanton was on the Pacers' team bus as it rolled down the highway for the 30-minute trip back to Aiken.

Clanton decided to drive home to Ohio after arriving back on campus. He hopped into his car and started off on the 589-mile drive to his home state. It was reported by media outlets in South Carolina Aiken head coach, Vincent Alexander, did not know Clanton planned to drive home right after the game. Earlier in the week, though, Clanton sent an email to professors letting them know he had to take care of a couple of things back home but he would be back on Monday. Clanton never made it to his destination.

Wednesday morning at 8:30, he fell asleep at the wheel along Interstate 77 North near Fairplain, W. Va. His car veered off the interstate, flipped at least once and Clanton was ejected from his car, which hit a tree. The car ended up in three sections, according to news reports, and Clanton was pronounced dead at the scene. Clanton had driven nearly 500 miles. He was only a couple of hours from home in Reynoldsburg, a suburban city outside of Columbus. Bostic learned, later that morning, the life of his childhood friend had ended in tragedy.

"I talked to him the day before he died and my brother actually talked to him that night," Bostic said. "When I got that call, it hurt. I was celebrating the Bellarmine victory from the night before. It was an emotional high. To go from that excitement to not being able to celebrate...It was hard. It was hard. I couldn't believe he was gone."

Bostic leaned on his unbreakable faith to get through the tragedy and, while it wasn't easy to go forward and focus on basketball, he knew, in his heart, Clanton would do the same. The Oilers were three wins away from a title and, although Bostic was dealing with the unimaginable pain of losing a close friend, he was determined to honor his him.

"I thought a lot about what Javonte would have done if he were in my position and I knew he would have gone to that tournament and balled out as hard as he could," Bostic said. "I played as hard as I could for him, played my butt off to win it all."

Bostic didn't get a chance to attend the funeral. It wasn't scheduled until the following Tuesday, when the Oilers would be on the road preparing for the Elite Eight. Bostic's dad, a minister, did the service for Clanton's funeral before heading to Springfield to watch his son play in the national tournament. While Bostic wasn't there to say goodbye before Clanton was laid to rest, he took the memory of his friend with him to Springfield. Bostic wrote Clanton's name on his shoes and thought about him every time he shot a free throw during the national tournament. It was his way of honoring a close friend and, playing in honor of Clanton, served as an added driving force in his quest to win a national championship

5 MEET THE TEAM

Findlay had the depth and talent to win a championship, its roster headlined by Bostic, who was coming off a year where he averaged just under 14 points per game and grabbed six rebounds per outing. A first-team All-GLIAC pick as well as an all-defensive team and all-region pick as a junior, Bostic was the most complete player in the country

He showed potential for greatness early in his career at Findlay, starting twenty-six of twenty-nine games as a freshman and averaging 8.6 points and 5.6 rebounds per game.

A year later, Bostic took steps forward, pushing his scoring average above eleven while improving his rebounding average as well, pushing it to 6.1 rebounds per game. He was also impressive from beyond the arc, nailing forty 3-pointers and shined on defense, tallying fifty-three steals to earn all-defensive team honors in the conference. He was a second-team all-conference selection, as well. His background as a football player would serve him well in his quest to help the Oilers win a championship, taking advantage of his football mentality from a physical standpoint.

Lewis entered his senior year on the heels of his best season as an Oiler, starting thirty-three games and earning second team All-GLIAC honors as he averaged 12.9 points per outing. There was little doubt he was the most athletic player on the team and his high-flying dunking ability dazzled fans time and again. He seemed to have unlimited potential coming out of high school where he was the Cleveland Plain Dealer of the Year and the Northeast Conference Player of the Year. It would take time, however, for to live up to his potential.

After scoring only 49 points as a freshman, Lewis played just ten games as a sophomore, starting only three times. Eligibility issues hurt his cause and, often, players throw in the towel when they deal with issues off the court. Lewis didn't let it happen, overcoming the adversity in his life, a credit to his determination and will to be the best he could be. That led to a remarkable junior season and set the stage for his stellar senior year.

Lee Roberts was a talented senior out of Midpark High in Northeast Ohio and was coming off a big junior season in which he scored in double figures twenty-two times and had a motor that never stopped running. He averaged nearly 12 points per game and was a great defender, blocking twenty-six shots, and earned a spot on the All-GLIAC team. Roberts also had background in track and was an indoor state champion in the high jump, while in high school and also competed for the track team at Findlay, winning the long jump title at the outdoor conference meet as a junior. The year before, Roberts qualified for the national meet and finished twelfth, his success providing a glimpse of how good of an athlete Roberts really was and he would take advantage of that athleticism time and again, during the 2008-09 season. Just as Lewis found it difficult to shine right away, Roberts also got off to a slow start, scoring only 79 points as a freshman. He saw action in thirty-one games the following year and averaged 6.8 points and 4.6 rebounds per game, while swatting away thirty-one shots, nearly tripling the total number of blocks he had as a freshman. Roberts would start twenty-seven games as a junior and he shot 63.3 percent from the floor, setting a school record for field goal percentage in a season.

The other two returning starters for the Oilers were senior guard, Tyler Evans, and junior point guard, Marcus Parker.

Evans played high school basketball at Logan Elm in Circleville. He arrived at Findlay fresh off a senior season where he was the Mid-State League Player of the Year. Evans also earned first-team All-Ohio honors as a junior and was a second team all-state selection as a senior. His prep career ended with the opportunity to play in the North/South All-Star Game in Columbus and he played well enough to earn MVP honors of the game. Evans played in all thirty games as a freshman and went on to play in every game of his collegiate career, setting a school record for most games played by a Findlay player. He certainly thrived in that first season with the Oilers as he showed of his 3-point shooting ability, knocking down thirty treys. Evans shot close to 50 percent from the outside that year and scored in double figures eight time. As a sophomore, Evans started two games. His scoring production slipped slightly as he made thirty-eight 3-pointers and averaged just under 6 points per game. He took his game to another level as a junior, stepping into a starting role for the Oilers. Evans started all thirty-three games and became more dangerous from the outside, knocking down sixty shots from 3-point range. Evans scored in double figures twelve times and tied his career-high for 3-pointers in a game, with six in a win over Lake Superior State. He also handed out twenty-four assists and racked up twenty-four steals.

Parker was the player who would run the show offensively. Arguably the most talented point guard I've seen play at Findlay; he came to the Oilers with an understanding of how to rise to the occasion in big games. Parker was a two-time Division I state champion at Canton McKinley High School and a third-team All-Ohio selection as a senior. I remember talking with him on the phone after he signed with the Oilers and he told me his goals were to be better than Pfeifer and to win a national championship.

A lot of players talk about what they want to accomplish in college, but talking about it and doing it are two different things. If there was anyone who could deliver on big promises, though, it was Parker, who always played with confidence. It didn't matter he stood just 5-foot-9-inches tall. What he lacked in height, he made up for it in talent, heart, and mental toughness. He lived up to the hype immediately, earning GLIAC Freshman of the Year honors and becoming the first in program history to earn D-II Bulletin Freshman All-American honors. Parker started twenty-nine games during his rookie season and averaged 9.0 points per game. He dished out 98 assists and was a solid defender, racking up sixty-one steals enroute to earning a spot on the league's all-defensive team. Parker drilled thirty-seven 3-pointers as a freshman and concerns of a sophomore slump faded quickly. Parker, who could score just as easily on a quick drive to the basket as he did pulling up from long range, started all thirty-three games and averaged just under 11 points per game. He punctuated his scoring effort by hitting fifty-three 3-pointers. Parker also handed out 133 assists and continued his tremendous play on defense as he racked up fifty-eight steals. His efforts earned him a spot on the GLIAC All-Defensive team and on the league's all-tournament team. Parker also made it on the NCAA regional all-tournament team and had every intention of doing his part to lead Findlay to a national title his junior year.

As important as the starters are to success, teams typically don't win championships if the role players didn't produce when called upon. Nathan Hyde was among those players. He was a local player out of Liberty-Benton, where he was the Division III Player of the Year as a senior. A two-time all-state pick in high school, Hyde wasted no time making his presence felt in college. He played in all thirty-three games as a freshman and shot better than 50 percent from the field while knocking down thirty-one 3-pointers and coming up with thirty-three steals. One of his greatest strengths was his ability to hit free throws and he quickly established himself as one of the top free throw shooters on the team and the conference, connecting on nearly 85 percent of his shots from the line. Some questioned whether Hyde was good enough to play Division II basketball when I mentioned to some that he was being recruited by the Oilers. It surprised me a little because I saw him play several times in his high school career and was convinced he was good enough.

Aaron Laflin was also going to be counted on to play a pivotal role off the bench. A backup point guard out of Pickerington North, Laflin was heading into his senior season with the Oilers. He came into school fresh off a senior year of high school where he was named the Ohio Capital Conference Player of the Year and an honorable mention All-Ohio selection. Laflin averaged 19 points, five rebounds and four assists as a senior at Pickerington North.

As do most freshmen, Laflin got off to a slow start, scoring only 32 points in twenty-four games but he made he made major strides as a sophomore, starting twice in thirty-one games and scoring in double figures three times, while hitting twenty 3-pointers and before handing out fifty-four assists. His value as a backup point guard to Parker was even more noticeable during his junior season when he averaged 4.8 points and played in thirty-two games. He knocked down twenty-six shots from beyond the arc that season and scored 10 or more points six times; making him a player the Oilers knew they could rely on when they needed him most. His experience, along with his ability to come into a game and keep the Oilers' offense running smoothly, was huge for a team with championship aspirations.

Sophomore forward, Tyler Sparks, was the hard-nosed, gutsy player every championship-caliber team needs. A star in football and basketball at Olmstead Falls High School in the Cleveland area, he was a two-time all-state player in both sports and was tabbed as the offensive player of the year in football in the Northeast District. Sparks was a consistent shooter his freshman year, hitting nearly 49 percent of his shots and he averaged 4.5 points while dishing out twenty-seven assists and tallying twenty-four steals. Not bad numbers for an athlete who could have just as easily played college football.

No one on the team epitomized toughness more than sophomore center, Jason Wehri, who battled non-Hodgkin's lymphoma as a sophomore at Ottoville High School in rural Putnam County. He played in a town roughly forty minutes west of Findlay and quickly became a crowd favorite when he arrived on campus. The fans admired his toughness, which shined through during his chemotherapy sessions every two weeks. Amazingly, he missed one practice in high school while battling cancer and that was because of a doctor's appointment. He never missed a game. It's tough enough to play a sport when you are healthy, so the fact that Wehri did it when he wasn't 100 percent, says a lot about his mental and physical toughness. Wehri ended up as a two-time All-Ohio honorable mention selection in high school and took that no-quit state of mind with him to Findlay. He scored 30 points in his first season and grabbed thirty-three rebounds as well but what made him so valuable was he never hesitated to step in front of a player driving to the basket to take a charge. Some of the hits he took made fans cringe but no matter how hard he fell, he always got up and went back to work. His blue-collar work ethic would serve him well in the season ahead.

Redshirt junior Nick Coon, sophomore forward Michael Agunga, redshirt freshman forward Antoine Wilhite, freshman forward Rob Marsden and freshman guard Justin Schomaeker rounded out the roster.

Coon was actually part of the recruiting class that included Bostic, Lewis, Roberts and Laflin, a heralded recruiting class that came to campus with great expectations. Unlike the other four, Coon did not play his freshman season. Coon played his high school basketball at Mount Vernon and was the Ohio Capital Conference Central Division Player of the Year as a senior. His high basketball IQ and versatility is what made him a great role player. After managing only 9 points as a redshirt freshman, he scored 40 the following season, the majority coming off nine 3-pointers.

As was Wehri, Agunga was one of the fan favorites, earning that label because he played hard every time he came off the bench. He scored a season-high 11 in games against Lake Superior State and Wayne State as a freshman and was eager to play even better as a sophomore. Agunga hailed from Grove City High School and was one of the better high school players in the Columbus area, as he earned first-team All-Ohio Capital Conference honors as a senior. His willingness to play hard, regardless of the number of minutes he played, would prove beneficial to the Oilers in the season ahead.

Marsden was from England and red-shirted during the 2008-09 season. During his senior year at Danum

School in Domcaster, he averaged 27.5 points and fourteen rebounds per game. He was the MVP of his team three times and was one of only twelve players to be selected to play on England's Under-20 national team. Marsden was also named one of the top five prospects for England's national squad.

Schomaeker had one of the more interesting stories when it came to role players. In high school, he played at Ottawa-Glandorf, located twenty minutes down the road from Findlay and considered one of the better programs in the state. It's also the same school Niekamp coached at during his days as a high school coach for a period of time. The Oilers had a reputation for recruiting primarily Ohio players and they often hit the local high school scene to find those players. Schomaeker came to Findlay as a walk-on, passing on a chance to play at a smaller school where he could have had an opportunity to play a bigger role right away. He was coming off a senior season in which he helped lead the Titans to a state championship, averaging 17.6 points and four rebounds per game and earning all-state honors. Schomaeker didn't play his first year at Findlay but did put himself in a position where he could win a national title just one year after winning a state championship.

Niekamp knew the season ahead was going to be different from any other in his previous twenty-three seasons with the Oilers. The pieces were in place for a championship run but the Oilers would go into it with the biggest bulls-eye they ever had on its back. The pressure that came with being No. 1, and the expectations attached to such a lofty ranking were not easy to handle but Niekamp was known for getting the most out of his players. He had won 514 games and only five seasons ended with ten or more losses. Seventeen times he won twenty or more games, including thirty in 2004-05. His worst record in the stretch was 14-13 in 1990-91. What made Niekamp a great coach is he knew which buttons to push. He wasn't one of those coaches who stood up the whole game and shouted at his team. He prepared his team to play during the week and he would spend the games sitting calmly on the bench, most of the time as the action unfolded in front of him. The moments when he stood up and burned a timeout were the ones where his players knew he meant business. They listened because they knew it was rare for Niekamp to get fired up and the players always responded well to Niekamp's instructions coming out of a timeout.

Niekamp was a star basketball player at St. Henry High School in Ohio and went on to play at Miami of Ohio, where he was a member of teams that made the NCAA and NIT tournaments. His first head coaching job was at Parkway High School in Ohio. He spent two seasons at the helm of the Panthers before taking a job at Ottawa-Glandorf. Niekamp guided the Titans to a pair of state tournament appearances in his five seasons and was named the Ohio High School Class AA Coach of the Year in 1977. His final stop in the high school ranks was Lima Senior, which was about thirty miles South of Findlay on Interstate 75. He spent six seasons at the school and led the Spartans to the 1982 state tournament. Niekamp won a total of 208 games as a high school coach and was given his first opportunity to coach college basketball in 1985, when he was hired by Findlay. It was the beginning of a remarkable career that would end in 2011, when he retired with more than 500 wins. Niekamp carried on a great tradition of Findlay basketball. Niekamp was just the third coach of the Oilers since 1947. Don Renninger coached eight seasons and won five Mid-Ohio titles. He guided Findlay to the NAIA national tournament twice. James Houdeshell took over in 1955 and would coach for thirty seasons, leading the Oilers to the NAIA national tourney three times.

The transition the Oilers made from NAIA to NCAA Division II proved to be a smooth one, as the Oilers went 20-9 in 1997-98, their first season at the Division II level. They won a GLIAC South Division title that season but because of the probationary period teams must go through when they move to a different level, the Oilers were not eligible for the NCAA postseason. The division crown was the first of seven the Oilers won over the next ten years. The Oilers also won the conference tournament three times in that stretch but a national championship had always been the ultimate goal and it seemed now Niekamp had the team that could deliver one.

Ernst, who is now the head coach of the Oilers, taking over in 2011, was considered one of the best assistant coaches in the country at the Division II level going into the 2008-09 season. He had opportunities to leave Findlay and take a more high-profile job but his loyalty to the Oilers was strong. Ernst was entering his eighteenth season as an assistant, including his seventh as the team's top assistant coach. He handled much of the recruiting process and was the coach players talked about in interviews when they mentioned the Oilers' success on defense. Ernst was from Ohio and played his high school basketball at Minster, where he was a two-time All-Midwest Athletic Conference selection. He played basketball for the Oilers as well and graduated in 1992. With his help, the Oilers earned a reputation for being one of the best defensive teams in the league and country and there was no question defense would play a crucial role in the Oilers' journey through a season of high expectations.

6 PLAYING WITH A HEAVY HEART

Lewis soared above the rim inside the Schottenstein Center in Columbus on a Thursday night in November of 2007, taking an assist from Bostic and throwing down a thunderous dunk in an exhibition game against Ohio State. Sitting in a wheelchair and trying to fight off the pain caused by the ugliness of cancer, John Lewis cheered for his son. The elder Lewis made his son a promise that he would live to see this game, the first one of the year for the Oilers, and he made good on that promise as he watched Morgan help the Oilers to a stunning 70-68 victory over the Buckeyes. The dunk made the top ten plays on SportsCenter that night on ESPN but an upset win over a Division I opponent isn't what made the night one Morgan would never forget. It was that his dad was there to see him play even though medical logic said he should have never been in the gym.

"He kept his promise of watching me play one more game, a special game where we upset The Ohio State University," Morgan said, as he recalled the vivid memories of that November night in Columbus. "He was in his wheelchair in the stands, and that was a moment of my basketball career I will never forget."

Seven months earlier, John had been diagnosed with lung cancer. Lewis was ineligible to play at UF at the time and there was no guarantee he would play for the Oilers the following season.

"I had a lot going on personally that year and ineligible during my sophomore season," Lewis said. "Thanks to the amazing coaching staff we had at Findlay, I did summer school and came back my junior season with the best grades I have ever had in school. We had a decent basketball season, too."

It shouldn't surprise anyone Morgan regained his eligibility and put himself in a position for his dad to see him play one more time. Unlike so many talented young athletes, Morgan was never pushed too hard by his father for the sake of achieving athletic glory. He was given a chance to be himself and, no matter what he chose to do in life; Morgan knew his father supported him 100 percent.

"My dad always let me be me," Morgan said. "The one thing now that I'm more mature is I've come to appreciate that my father never pushed me into anything except getting good grades. My father didn't care if I was a firefighter, a teacher, a karate instructor or even a professional basketball player. My father let me do what made me happy and he supported me with all he had. As long as I was smiling, he was smiling."

It was hard to find a reason to smile after the cancer diagnosis but that promise meant something more than words could ever describe. While the odds were against John being able to keep his promise, he was going to find a way to defy them and be in a gym to cheer on his son again.

"The doctor gave him four to six weeks to live after he was diagnosed but my father promised me he would watch me play one more game before he died," Morgan said. "After the cancer originated in his lungs, my father fought to stay alive as the cancer spread to his liver, kidneys and eventually bones. He couldn't walk, stand or even sleep."

It seemed as if John would lose his battle within the four- to six-week timeframe. It didn't seem possible a man could fight for his life against an unforgiving disease or live through the indescribable pain beyond the timeframe the doctor gave him; yet he carried on, pushing forward with all he had to keep a promise. One night, Morgan saw first-hand just how difficult the fight really was for his father.

"I came home one night from school to surprise my family and my dad was crying on the couch," Morgan said. "He didn't know I was coming home. I asked Mom about it and she told me he cries every night from the pain in his bones."

It was difficult for Morgan to watch his father fight his battle but he also learned valuable lessons from it, including fighting for what you want, no matter what. There were no tears of pain for one night in Columbus. Inside an arena buzzing with excitement, John was smiling because he was blessed with a chance to watch his son play basketball one final time. Morgan was smiling, too, thankful to have his father in the crowd and thankful his dad was able to keep a promise that provided him with a lesson he would never forget.

"I learned if you want something and can subconsciously believe it to be true, anything is possible," Morgan said.

Morgan still remembers seeing his dad after the game. They shared a hug before Morgan got on the bus for the trip home. As Morgan soaked in the importance of being able to have his dad at the game while on the ride home, John was taken back to Painesville. Two days later, he suffered a heart attack. He slipped into a coma and passed away a few days later. Bostic was there for Lewis during the difficult time and attended the funeral with him, another example of how close Bostic and Lewis had become since the beginning of their careers at Findlay. Morgan appreciated the fact that Bostic was just as good of a friend off the court as he was on it. He also appreciated the sacrifice his father made to see him play.

"The whole time he knew he would watch me play one more time, no matter what the doctor said," Morgan told me in an interview. "He knew what he wanted. The motto to my life: 'Thoughts become things'."

Morgan continued to live by that motto and, while he and his Findlay teammates fell short of a title in 2007-08, he never quit believing a championship was possible. He was ready to make that dream a reality during his senior season and, along the way, he would keep the memory of his father in his heart.

7 SETTING THE STAGE FOR TITLE RUN

The odds were not in Findlay's favor that it would remain the No. 1 team in the country the entire season. Cal State Bakersfield was the last to go wire-to-wire as the No. 1 team and win a title, accomplishing the feat in 1993. Other than Fort Hays State, the only other unbeaten champion in the history of Division II was Evansville in 1965. The Aces went 29-0 just eight years after the first tournament was played. Findlay wears a target on its back because of its reputation as one of the most successful Division II programs in the nation and opponents always seem to bring their A game against the Oilers. A No. 1 ranking was going to motivate their opponents even more.

Findlay entered the 2008-09 season having won twenty or more games in twelve consecutive seasons and had racked up twenty-one 20-win seasons in the last twenty-seven years. That said, did I think Findlay could win a national championship in 2009?

Absolutely. Did I think the Oilers could do it without losing a game and maintaining the No. 1 ranking for an entire year? Deep down, I hoped for it but I figured, at some point, the Oilers were probably going to lose a game. The biggest concern was having to play every team in their conference twice. The conference slate included two trips to the Upper Peninsula of Michigan, commonly called the UP by Michiganders. Life in the GLIAC can be rugged at times and, in some cases, the more physical team triumphs over the more talented team. Surviving a twenty-two-game conference schedule appeared to be mission impossible, although the Oilers did run the table in the league in 2006-07 when they finished 17-0.

The Oilers seemed to handle the added hype quite well, with the No. 1 ranking rarely mentioned, and they showed no fears about the challenges ahead. It was almost as if they embraced everything that came with the territory of being the favorite. Niekamp had a lot to do with keeping Findlay focused. He had been a coach long enough to know that being No. 1 at the start of the season can weigh heavily on the shoulders of a team.

"We felt we would be ranked high but No. 1 was something we didn't plan on," Niekamp said, before the start of the season. "We have to find a way to make that a plus as opposed to a burden. If you go back to last year, we did a lot of good things, but we didn't achieve our first goal, which was to win the GLIAC South. We have to go back to the basics and get better as a team. The memory of last year should be a motivator."

Still, remaining No. 1 was going to be difficult.

"We are going to bring out the best in everyone," Niekamp said. "We have to take that as a challenge and prove we deserve to be No. 1. There are probably people who question it. We need to use it as motivation."

Motivation wasn't going to be a problem for the Oilers, not when their loss to the Lakers in the Sweet 16 was still fresh in their minds. Staying on task wasn't going to be an issue.

"We are using last year as a learning experience," Bostic said. "It feels great to be No. 1 but we didn't win anything last year. We know before we can honestly look at winning a national championship, we have to focus on winning the GLIAC South title."

At Findlay, the division title was where success began to be measured. It was the title the Oilers used to lay the foundation for success in the postseason because winning the title meant Findlay was in a better position to win a conference tournament title and earn a higher seed in the NCAA tournament. In 2008, the Oilers were denied a division championship. They headed into the 2008-09 season aiming for their eighth crown in program history.

"I think we are being careful about putting the cart before the horse," Niekamp said. "You can talk about a lot of other things but, if we don't win the GLIAC South, we don't go anywhere. It sets up opportunities for us in the postseason. It is our main focus."

Lewis said the South Division was, no doubt, the first goal on the team's mind yet he couldn't help but think about the possibility of being a national champion. "Our No. 1 goal, right now, is to win the GLIAC South Division title," Lewis said, in a preseason interview. "Winning a national championship is in the back of our minds but we can't look ahead. We have to take it practice by practice and game by game. We have to stay away from the hype. It's an honor to be the preseason No. 1 but we can't get big heads. We have to work hard. It should be a fun year."

The Oilers appreciated the preseason recognition; if they were to survive the journey, though, it was going to take a heck of an effort.

"We feel blessed because not many players get to be in the situation we are in," Bostic said. "The No. 1 ranking is a compliment to our program but, like you said, it's a bullseye. We have to come out and play every game like it's a championship game. If we want to get to where we want to go, we have to suck it up and play hard every day and know better things are coming. We definitely want to go out with a bang."

8 EXHIBITION SHOWDOWN WITH XAVIER

Lewis shared an interesting thought, as he and I talked after practice a few days before the Oilers' exhibition showdown with Xavier.

"We want to make sure Niekamp has to coach us in the last five minutes of the game and not just sit there on the bench with his legs crossed," Lewis said in an interview. "We expect to give Xavier a good game. We're looking forward to it."

Games against Division I opponents were the norm for Findlay. In past seasons, the Oilers played Bowling Green, Ohio State, Dayton, Miami of Ohio, and Utah. Giving Xavier a good game wasn't going to be easy because the Musketeers were coming off a school-record 30-win season and second appearance in the Elite Eight in the last five seasons. Xavier had played in eighteen of the last twenty-six NCAA tournaments and was going into the 2008-09 season with the usual lofty expectations.

Derrick Brown was its headline player and entered

the year as a projected late first-round pick in the NBA Draft. None of the hype draped over the Musketeers intimidated the Oilers, though, who were anxious to take their best shot inside the Cintas Center in Cincinnati on the night of November 7. Bostic welcomed the challenge Xavier would present. Bostic was like every other athlete; his dream was to play at the Division I level. He just never got his shot. This game against Xavier was his chance to make a statement, to prove he was more than capable of holding his own against Division I athletes. For a team like Findlay, this battle with Xavier was an opportunity to not only play under a brighter spotlight but an opportunity to learn about itself as a team.

"I used to always watch Xavier on T.V. It's going to be exciting to play against them," Bostic said. "We look forward to playing the bigger schools. It gives us a chance to get in the limelight a little and allows us to see what we need to work on to improve as a team."

Winning wasn't nearly as important as what the Oilers would gain from the experience, which is why Niekamp worked hard to schedule a couple of exhibition games each season.

"Xavier will exploit our weaknesses quickly," Niekamp said. "They will help us learn what we need to work on to be a better team."

Game day arrived and music blared inside the Cintas Center, as the Oilers warmed up in front of a hostile crowd for their much-anticipated showdown with the Musketeers. Fans taunted the Oilers as they launched up shots during pregame warm-ups. The Oilers weren't here to be a sacrifice but they looked like one early on. Bostic, the player expected to shine in this moment, couldn't make a shot to save his life during a miserable opening half. He missed all four of his attempts from the floor and picked up three fouls. His teammates weren't much better off. Findlay shot a chilly 25.9 percent from the floor, hitting on only seven of its twenty-seven attempts. Frustration was setting in quickly in front of a raucous crowd of 7,865. It didn't get much better as the half wore on and the Oilers found themselves in a 37-23 hole at halftime.

"The first half was super frustrating," Bostic said. "When you are throwing up bricks like I was, you start questioning yourself but I knew if I was patient, I would get through it."

Bostic's patience paid off. He got rolling in the second half and started showcasing the skills that made him the favorite to be the National Player of the Year in Division II. Bostic finished the night with 23 points and four steals. Despite a valiant effort, Findlay's hope for a win was fading fast. Eleven minutes remained and Xavier led 55-39. B.J. Raymond, who scored 17 points, played a pivotal role in helping the Musketeers build their lead. His two 3-pointers, along with a dunk by Brown, fueled an 8-2 run that put Xavier in front by 16. The Oilers had no intentions of calling it a day and crept back into the game behind a stellar defensive effort. Defense has always been the backbone of Findlay basketball and, on this night, good defense would put the Oilers in a position to win. Findlay began forcing turnovers and making shots for the Musketeers much more difficult to come by. Xavier turned the ball over twenty-eight times in all on the night but managed to stay in front because it shot close to 60 percent.

With 4:51 to play, the Oilers were within striking distance, putting the pressure on the Musketeers to respond. Xavier stayed a step ahead of Findlay, barely, as Bostic came up with a steal with six seconds to play that cut the Xavier lead to 78-76. Raymond split a pair of free throws on the other end to put the Musketeers up 79-76. Parker was determined to keep Findlay's shot for a win alive. He attempted a 3-pointer at the buzzer in the hopes of sending the game into overtime. The ball bounced off the rim as time expired, allowing Xavier to escape with the three-point victory. The Oilers hardly came away from the thrilling showdown empty-handed. Lewis' wish came true. Niekamp had to coach in the last five minutes and, afterwards, the veteran coach of the Oilers talked about his team's tremendous effort.

"We were able to get something going in the second half," Niekamp said, in an interview outside his team's locker room. "We moved the ball around more and worked for good shots. Our goal was to compete with a top-level Division I program. We did that. It was important to our players to make this a competitive game."

Several Oilers played well, including Lewis, who poured in 16 points and grabbed six rebounds. His highlight moment was a thunderous one-handed dunk over Brown in the lane that rattled the Xavier star. Lewis made it known he was pretty good too, coming through with a highlight-worthy play and it was obvious Brown wasn't happy. Roberts pumped in 10 points and Parker and Evans scored 9 points apiece. Although the Oilers were ultimately hoping for a win, they left Cincinnati late Friday night with an extra dose of confidence that would serve them well as they prepared to turn their attention toward the start of their season.

"We didn't think Xavier was better than us," Roberts said in a post-game interview. "We can take this as a learning experience. We will watch the video of the game, see what we did wrong and take those lessons into the season."

The game could have become ugly in a hurry but the Oilers handled themselves well in a hostile environment. They responded like a championship-caliber team and their gutsy effort against Xavier added to the excitement that was building for a special season.

9 SEASON OPENER

Findlay came into its regular-season opener against the University of Indianapolis as owners of a fifty-eight-game home win streak and had not lost a regular season game at Croy Gymnasium since Feb. 12, 2004, when it was tripped up by Gannon in a 70-68 setback. The only other loss at home during the stretch was to Northern Kentucky in the 2007 NCAA tournament.

Croy Gymnasium is electric when it's sold out. The fans are passionate and knowledgeable and they roar to life when the Oilers are rolling against an opponent. It is one of the best small-college basketball atmospheres in the country but Findlay's home court dominance would be put to the test by the Greyhounds out of the Great Lakes Valley Conference on the night of Nov. 18.

Indy hailed from the rival league of the GLIAC in the Midwest Region and no one had to remind the Oilers of the challenge in front of them. "Indy is a highly regarded program and they will come ready to play," Niekamp said, in an interview the day before the game. "They won't come in unprepared." The fact that the Greyhounds would not be a pushover was all the more reason for Niekamp to be thankful his team would get to play this non-conference showdown at home. "It's nice to be starting off at home. There is no question we have played well at home over the years and we hope that advantage will help us," Niekamp said.

The Greyhounds and Oilers last met in 2004 in the NCAA regional at Lewis University in Romeoville, Ill. Findlay prevailed in that opening-round game, edging Indy 84-83 in overtime. The Greyhounds had played a rigorous exhibition schedule prior to the start of their regular season, facing off against the University of Tennessee and Indiana University-Purdue University. The Greyhounds lost 87-73 to the Volunteers and were beaten 83-75 by the Jaguars. The Greyhounds also had one game in the regular season under their belt as they rolled over Taylor University 104-65 in their opener. Senior guard Tyler Cockerham and senior forward Jordan Barnard were Indy's top players, returning from a team that went 14-13 the previous season. Cockerham averaged 8.4 points per game in 2007-08 and was Indy's top returning scorer. The showdown between the Oilers and Greyhounds had added significance because of the weight it carried in the long run for the NCAA tournament selection process.

"This game has a lot of significance," Niekamp said. "It's an important opening game for us and we need to play our best to win."

Game night arrived and Findlay, as expected, had its hands full against Indy, which hung around early before the Oilers surged in front by 6 points on the strength of a 15-4 run. Sparks fueled the run, coming in off the bench to hit a few clutch shots, grab a couple of important rebounds and rack up a few steals during the outburst. His highlight moment was a dunk he threw down after driving the baseline to put the Oilers up 17-11 with thirteen minutes to play in the opening half. The Oilers went into halftime with a 36-23 advantage after shooting 44.1 percent from the field but could not take the life out of the Greyhounds. Indy trimmed its deficit to 46-40 with 14:35 left and was determined to make things a little too close for comfort. The momentum did not last, as the Oilers roared to life with an avalanche of big-time shots, including a clutch 3-pointer by Hyde and thunderous dunks by Bostic and Lewis. Findlay also came up with several key defensive stops during a 19-8 run that appeared to be enough to break the backs of the Greyhounds. With nine minutes to play, hope seemed to be fading for Indy, which trailed 65-48. Its hopes were revived when Keith Radcliff, who poured in 20 points, nailed a jumper with a little over four minutes to play, cutting the Oilers' lead to 66-62.

Rather than wilt under the pressure, the Oilers embraced it and cranked up its intensity on defense, while connecting on seven of its eight attempts from the free-throw line down the stretch. Sparks helped put the exclamation point on the 77-66 victory with a two-hand dunk on a fast break in the final minute to energize the crowd one last time on opening night. Sparks finished with 14 points and six rebounds.

"I am always going to give 110 percent because I never know how much playing time I am going to get," Sparks said, in a post-game interview inside a jubilant Findlay locker room. "We have a lot of good players on our team and they open up things for our role players. That's what happened tonight."

The Findlay way has always been to force opponents to pick their poison and, on this night, it was Sparks who took advantage of the Greyhounds' mistake of overlooking him.

"Tyler is a gritty player and he always gives us that type of effort," Niekamp said. "He does a lot of the things that make a difference."

Indy shot a respectable 48.1 percent from the field and the Oilers didn't fare too well from beyond the arc, connecting on only three of their fifteen attempts.

"This was a grind it out type of game," Niekamp said, inside his office during a postgame interview. "We extended the lead several times but they got right back into the game. To their credit, they didn't roll over."

The Oilers showed off their potential as well, at times. They were relentless on defense, forcing nineteen turnovers and balanced offensively as six players scored in double figures. Roberts was one of them. He dropped in 14 points, pulled down seven rebounds and blocked two shots. Bostic scored 13 points and the fact that he didn't lead the team in scoring said a lot about the Oilers' depth. Lewis scored 12 points. Parker finished with 11 points and Hyde added 10 as Findlay took down the Greyhounds, who had only two players score 10 or more points. Roberts was happy with how the Oilers handled themselves in a big game, especially late, and did not undersell the importance of playing this one at home.

"In the end, we started playing like a team and found a way to get through it," Roberts said outside the Findlay locker room. "Our atmosphere tonight was a huge part of the game. They say home-court advantage is worth 10 points and, basically, it was for us."

Roberts played a pivotal role in making that home-court advantage work in the Oilers' favor. Roberts always played with energy that bordered on beyond intense and, while he didn't need to lead Findlay in scoring every night or even be one of the top three scorers, he did know it was important to play hard every minute.

"I need to come ready to play every night," Roberts said. "I play with a lot of emotion and try to be as aggressive on defense as possible because defense is what this team is all about."

Niekamp thought the balanced effort was crucial to the team's success against the Greyhounds and depth was going to be key going forward for the Oilers in their quest to win a title.

"It's a big win in the region against a very good team," Niekamp said. "Do we have things we can improve on? Yes. There are a lot of things but it was a good effort and we can build on it as we go forward."

The win over the Greyhounds was the first step in the right direction, although there was no question, this team still had work to do, if it was going to fulfill its ultimate dream.

10 RUNNING WITH THE RACERS

Before Findlay made the jump to D-II in the late 1990s, it was one of the most successful NAIA programs in the nation. The Oilers made the playoffs thirty-three times between 1952 and 1999, reaching the national tournament eleven times, with six of those appearances coming under the guidance of Niekamp. As a result of their deeply rooted history in NAIA, the Oilers made an effort to schedule at least one NAIA opponent each season.

The University of Northwestern Ohio, located in Lima Ohio, which is about thirty minutes south of Findlay, was selected as the Oilers' opponent this time. The school had revived its hoops program in 2007, marking the first time since the 1986-87 campaign that it had a team. Back then, however, Northwestern was a two-year school. It t had grown decidedly in the last two decades and Chris Adams, a long-time high school coach at Elida, which is just down the road from Northwestern, was in charge of

55

leading the program, while also serving as the school's athletic director. Adams spent twenty-one seasons at Elida and was 380-189 but success wasn't going to be as easily obtained at Northwestern. In his first season with the Racers, Northwestern finished 9-19. Year two didn't start off much better, as the Racers headed to Findlay for a Nov. 21 game with a 2-3 record, in the grip of a two-game losing streak.

Josh Vorst, a former star at Ottoville High School, was the leading scorer for Northwestern and came into the game against the Oilers averaging 15.2 points per game. In a loss to Malone two nights earlier, Vorst scored 16 points. On paper, this looked like a glorified scrimmage, as Northwestern lacked the talent and athleticism to keep pace with the Oilers.

Through one half of play, the Racers were in the game. They never led but did get within 10 several times before going into halftime down 42-30. They were able to stay in the game because Bostic struggled to get on track early on. No player was playing with higher expectations and pressure than Bostic because of his status as the preseason National Player of the Year but this was a night where he couldn't get into a rhythm. He took five shots and connected only once, as he finished the first half with only four points. Bostic wasn't thrilled. Neither was Niekamp.

"Coach Niekamp got on me at halftime about playing harder and being a leader," Bostic told me, in a post-game interview. "He wanted me to get after it on both ends of the floor."

Bostic responded as well as any player could have after such a miserable start, scoring 11 points in the first five minutes of the second half and his determined effort helped the Oilers jump out to a 62-44 lead with thirteen minutes to play. Bostic finished his night shooting 6-of-11 from the floor, lighting up the Racers for 23 points. Stellar play on the defensive end of the floor helped fuel the Oilers' second-half success, with one play in particular breaking the Racers' last ounce of spirit.

Northwestern's Jason Sarno tried to drive into the lane and score on a layup but Parker swatted the shot away. The ball ended up in the hands of Bostic, who sprinted down the floor and lobbed it into the air for Lewis. Lewis soared toward the basket from the left baseline and threw down a dunk for a 55-35 lead. His ferocious jam dazzled the crowd of 1,345 and was the highlight of his 14-point effort. Bostic and Lewis hooked up on that type of play often in their careers, especially as seniors, and their effort in the second half wasn't unnoticed.

"I thought Josh and Morgan picked up their level of intensity," Niekamp said, in a post-game interview.

Adams could only shake his head in amazement as the Oilers dominated the second half enroute to an 80-59 win. His Racers found it impossible to slow down the Oilers' offensive attack and failed to find consistency in their own offense, turning the ball over twenty-three times, including twelve times in the second half. Vorst scored 19 points to pace the Racers. The Oilers shot close to 45 percent from the floor and used a balanced effort to secure the win. Roberts and Parker scored 11 points apiece as Findlay pushed its home win streak to 60.

"Findlay has a special team," said Adams, adding he was thankful the Oilers gave his team a chance to play this game because the experience would benefit it in the long run. "They have great chemistry and are very athletic. It was an against-all-odds situation for us but I thought we competed hard and we will learn from this experience."

The Oilers were far from perfect, turning the ball over sixteen times and hitting only eight of their twenty-two attempts from beyond the arc. "We're not shooting the ball as well as we are capable of shooting it," Niekamp said as we wrapped up our interview. "Your team plays with more energy if you are consistent on the offensive end and we haven't been consistent yet."

Bostic didn't disagree with those comments. "We aren't anywhere near where we need to be as a team," Bostic said. "We have a lot of work to do and we are focused on improving as a team every time we play."

11 STORM WARNING

November was about to come to close with the Oilers playing a non-conference game against Lake Erie College, Nov. 25. The Oilers were facing a Storm team that was 1-3 and in its first season of Division II basketball. Findlay and Lake Erie had met seven times in the past and the Oilers had won every time. I talked with Coon that week and featured him in my game preview. He had been a successful player at the high school level and a valuable role player for Findlay, especially in that Laflin was out with a broken foot. Coon only scored four points and dished out four assists in the first two games but the stats weren't nearly as important as his ability to handle the backup point guard duties.

"You never know when you are going to be called upon and I've always been ready to step up, if needed," Coon said. "I feel comfortable filling in for Aaron. I get a chance to go up against some of the best players in the country every day in practice and that has prepared me for playing in games."

Every championship team needs players who are ready to play at a high level at any given time. Coon's versatility and high basketball IQ made him a player the Oilers could count on.

"He is a smart player who makes good decisions," Niekamp said, in an interview the week of the game against the Storm. "He can play the 1, 2 or 3 position and is getting the game experience he needs to grow as a player."

As for the looming game against the Storm, the Oilers didn't need to be reminded their next opponent wasn't going to be a pushover. Lake Erie had given No. 11 Grand Valley State all it could handle in a 65-63 loss, earlier in the month and were coming off a 50-46 win over California, PA. Derrick Thornton was the Storm's top player, averaging 14.8 points per game.

"Their game against Grand Valley was an eye opener," Niekamp said. "In a lot of ways, though, we are still focusing on what we need to do to build momentum and become more consistent. We have a lot we can improve on."

Swish.

Just like that, another 3-pointer cut through the net off the hand of Hyde as the Oilers got rolling against the Storm. Hyde's third trey of the game helped fuel an 18-4 run to break the spirit of the Storm and bring the crowd inside Croy Gymnasium roaring to its feet. Those treys by Hyde, one of the better shooters on the team, helped push the Findlay lead to 25-9 with 10:57 remaining in the opening half.

"I was able to find the gaps and my teammates were able to find me for open shots," Hyde said, of his sizzling first-half effort. "Every time I come off the bench, I try to be a spark, whether it's scoring points or playing good defense. I was lucky enough to hit big shots."

The Oilers hit eight 3-pointers in the first half, the last by Evans with eight seconds to play, as they rolled into halftime with a 52-30 advantage. Findlay was able to burn the Storm from the outside because Roberts did a phenomenal job of making life miserable for Lake Erie in the paint. He scored 9 points in the first seven minutes and the attention the Storm paid to Roberts left it vulnerable to the outside shot.

"Lee established himself inside and created opportunities for our shooters," Niekamp said. "Those 3-pointers allowed us to get a little separation."

The second half was a formality on a night when the Oilers shot 51.8 percent from the field. It was the first time all season Findlay shot better than 50 percent and Bostic dominated as he poured in 21 points, leading the Oilers to an 84-55 victory. Lewis dropped in 14 points and pulled down six rebounds, highlighting his effort with a rim-rocking dunk on a fast break with 16:21 to go, leaving Lake Erie staring up at a 57-34 deficit. The Oilers led by as many as 21 and got 13 points from Hyde and 11 points out of Roberts. Lake Erie turned the ball over seventeen times, overwhelmed by Findlay's aggressive defensive effort. The Storm shot just 39 percent from the field and Thornton managed only 9 points. The final twenty-seven minutes of the game were the toughest for the Storm, which made only nine field goals during the stretch.

Lewis wasn't impressed with the effort Findlay put forth defensively in the first month of the season. He admitted, after the game, the performance against the Storm was an encouraging sign.

"On film, we've looked like a preschool team on defense," Lewis said. "It doesn't even look like we're playing great, especially being a veteran team. We took strides in the right direction tonight."

Niekamp agreed the Oilers took a big step forward. The convincing victory put an exclamation point on November and, with conference play set to begin, the Oilers needed an effort like the one they gave against Lake Erie each night the rest of the way.

"We wanted to play zone against them and I thought we were pretty successful at it," Niekamp said, after the game. "We have steadily improved on defense. It feels good to get a decisive win before we start conference play next week."

Three straight wins to open the season was a good thing but Bostic and Lewis knew as well as anyone the road ahead would get more challenging.

"It's all about staying mentally ready, staying out of trouble, and keeping our minds right," Lewis said. "Like coach Niekamp has said, we've gone through every drill in practice. It's just a matter of executing in games. If we do that and stay focused, we should be fine."

The Oilers maintained their focus through three games, all against opponents they were expected to beat. Now, focus would become more important as the Oilers entered conference play. Those teams were familiar with Findlay and had the added motivation of trying to knock off the top-ranked team in the country. Lewis wasn't concerned. He was confident in what he and his teammates could accomplish in the weeks ahead as they prepared to reach their first goal, which was to win the South Division of the GLIAC.

"We're ready," Lewis said, without a hint of hesitation in his voice. "Every team is coming for us but we are ranked No. 1 and we are going to go out and give it our all. The other teams are coming for us, but we are coming for them, too. We have a lot of confidence. We want to play hard and take care of business. We will play every game like it is our last."

The Oilers not only had the drive to be the best, but they had tremendous team chemistry, which was evident in the first month of the season. They also had, arguably, the best coaching staff in the league, a staff that would put the Oilers in a position to succeed every time they took the floor.

"We have great coaches here and we also have great players," Bostic said. "As long as we continue to grow in each practice, we will be fine. Our chemistry is there, too. It makes it easier to play when the guy across from you knows what you are going to do before you do it. We have a deep team, too. It's scary how deep we are. I think that depth brings out the best in us."

In three games, fans were offered a glimpse of what the best from the Oilers looked like. Everyone had a feeling, however, that the best was yet to come.

12 GLIAC OPENER: SAGINAW VALLEY STATE

The GLIAC is one of the most competitive leagues in the country, and yet, it seems to lack the national respect other conferences receive, especially within the Midwest Region. It didn't matter Grand Valley State was coming off back-to-back appearances in the Elite Eight or that Findlay had played in an Elite Eight in 2005. The GLVC was still the powerhouse conference in the region. At least for this season, the GLIAC featured the team to beat. Findlay had won the South Division of the conference seven times and had three GLIAC tournament championships in its trophy case as well. The Oilers were the measuring stick for other teams in the league, a model of consistency.

The Oilers fell short of their usual standards the year before, coming up empty in their bid to win a division title and a league tournament crown. The disappointment served as added motivation in conference play. Saginaw Valley State, which is located in University Center, Mich., was up first on the league schedule. The Cardinals, projected to be a middle-of-the-pack team in the league, came to town for a Dec. 1 game seeking their first win. The Cardinals were 0-2 but the Oilers couldn't afford to look past Saginaw.

"We have to take every conference game seriously and go out and play like it's our last one," Lewis said, in an interview after practice the week of the Saginaw game. "Every team is going to come at us hard but, at the same time, we're going to give them our best shot, too."

That Findlay would be ready to be at its best is what concerned second-year Saginaw Valley head coach, Frankie Smith, the most. Smith was one of my favorite opposing coaches. A year earlier, in a game against the Oilers, he started talking to me while the game was going on and joked that he was thirsty. He picked up my bottle of Coke and a referee gave him a technical foul for it. I'm not sure why Smith was given a technical. He was just having a little fun as the final minutes played out in a game his team had no chance of winning. As for the upcoming game, Smith knew his team had the odds stacked against it. Findlay was averaging 80.3 points and giving up only 60.

"Findlay is a great team," Smith said, in a phone interview the week of the game. "They have a great offense, they are great in transition, they play great defense and they have a deep bench. We know we need to be at our best Thursday night."

The Cardinals, led by freshman guard Greg Foster, who was averaging 17.5 points per game, were coming off a 76-44 loss to sixth-ranked Northern Kentucky.

"Saginaw has a lot of talented players, especially at the guard position," Niekamp said. "We know this game will be a challenge and we put a lot of emphasis on conference games because we want to be in a position to win a division title."

I talked with Lewis in practice during the week about his progression as a player. He had scored in double figures in each of the first three games, picking up where he left off a year ago, when he scored in double figures twenty-two times. While his offensive improvements were impressive, he had made big steps forward as a defensive player, too. In three games, Lewis had racked up a team-best ten steals.

"I try to be one of our team's lock-down defenders," Lewis said. "When the ball goes to the man I'm guarding, I'm going to be a stopper. I take a lot of pride in the way I play defense."

Lewis was ready to go. So were the rest of the Oilers. Their quest to be the best team in the GLIAC was set to begin but a change in the starting lineup was in motion for the game against the Cardinals. Evans, a team captain, had been a starting guard for the first three games but Hyde had started off his sophomore season on a roll and replaced Evans in the starting lineup, a move Niekamp believed would prove beneficial to Hyde and Evans, who was held scoreless in the opener before scoring nine against Northwestern and six against Lake Erie.

"Nate has been playing so well and we thought bringing Tyler off the bench would help him get going a bit," Niekamp said of the decision that would set the stage for an interesting storyline down the road. "I thought he brought a lot of energy to the team on the defensive end and we need guys who can do that off the bench."

Hyde didn't miss a beat as a starter, dropping in 13 points against the Cardinals in an 83-58 victory. He remained a starter the rest of the season. Evans scored 8 points and played particularly well on defense, helping to defend against the Cardinals' talented cast of guards. Foster, Lawrence Ross, Dante Williams, and Avery Stephenson combined for 46 points, with only two coming from Foster, the team's leading scorer. Evans talked about his new role off the bench and the effort he gave against Saginaw Valley.

"Their guards are really quick and they all know how to score," Evans said. "It was going to take a team effort to slow them down. I thought I came out and played with confidence and did what I could to help. It was different coming off the bench but it was an easy adjustment."

While Evans adjusted to being a valuable player off the bench, it was business as usual for Bostic, who lit up the Cardinals for 19 points, marking the third consecutive game he scored 19 or more. He also pulled down seven rebounds and racked up four steals. It was Bostic who got the Oilers going against Saginaw Valley, who lost for the twelfth consecutive time to Findlay. He stole the ball two minutes into the game to tie the score at 2-2. Moments later, Bostic nailed a 3-pointer that pushed the Oilers' advantage to 8-3.

"Josh is a tough matchup," Niekamp said. "He can handle the ball, muscle up people inside and shoot it on the perimeter."

Bostic was never one to absorb all of the credit

and remained remarkably humble despite the hype surrounding him.

"I give props to the team because there isn't one guy you can focus on," Bostic said, in a post-game interview. "That frees me up in certain situations. It just happens I'm getting opportunities but, on any given night, the last guy on our bench can step up and have a big night."

Williams drained a 3-pointer for the Cardinals to slice the Oilers' lead to 30-24 with four minutes to go. Findlay was never seriously threatened and led 41-34 at halftime. The Oilers put the game out of reach in the second half on the strength of a quick scoring outburst by Hyde. The sophomore guard knocked down a couple of 3-pointers and drove into the lane for a layup while drawing contact as he went up for the shot. He hit the ensuing free throw to finish off a run of nine points in six minutes. His effort gave the Oilers a 57-39 lead. Saginaw Valley had no answer for the Oilers, who shot 50 percent from the field and hit nine treys while forcing twenty-four turnovers. The Cardinals, paced by the 20-point performance of Ross, shot 45.5 percent from the floor and gave up thirteen offensive rebounds. They went cold in the final ten minutes of action, making only three field goals on a night when scoring opportunities were few and far between.

"Defense is something we can always bring," Evans said. "Some nights the shots are falling and sometimes they aren't but we know we can play good defense every night."

The Oilers were thrilled about their latest win and another step of the journey was complete. "It feels good to get the first GLIAC win," Bostic said. "It's the first step on the ladder of what we hope is a long season."

13 BATTLE WITH LAKE SUPERIOR STATE

Findlay's final test of the first week of December was a battle with Lake Superior State on Dec. 3 at Croy Gymnasium. The Oilers were determined to not only protect their home floor but to crank up their defensive effort a few notches, as well.

"Coach has been yelling at us about playing better defense," Lewis said. "He told us because we're so athletic and so experienced, we should be able to take our defense to another level."

Findlay responded to the challenge. The Oilers opened the game on a 19-2 run as the Lakers struggled to get open looks. A total of nineteen turnovers did nothing to help their cause against the Oilers, nor did it help they had no answer for Roberts. The senior scored 8 points during the fiery start, including 2 points on a tip-in off a missed shot that put the Oilers on top 17-2. Findlay was threatened briefly later in the half, as Micah Hudson knocked down consecutive 3-pointers to trim the Oilers' advantage to 22-14 with eight minutes remaining. Hudson connected again from long range moments later, leaving Findlay scrambling to get a grip on the momentum, as its lead was sliced to 24-20. Findlay regained its composure and closed the half on a 10-0 run for a 34-20 advantage. The Oilers didn't miss a beat to start the second half as they used a 19-6 run early on. The outburst was fueled by five 3-pointers as Hyde and Parker got hot from the outside and propelled the Oilers to an 84-53 win. Hyde, making his second career start, drilled three treys during the run and finished with 12 points. It was his fourth time in double figures. Parker scored 10 points as the Oilers pushed their record to 5-0. That Lake Superior battled back in the first half to make things interesting did not surprise Parker.

"Every GLIAC team is going to make a run," Parker said, in a post-game interview. "We expected it but we know how to bounce back."

The Lakers shot only 36 percent from the field and Hudson scored 16 points. Unfortunately for Lake Superior, it lacked the athleticism to keep pace with the Oilers and didn't have the confidence Findlay had been playing with since the beginning of the season. Good teams thrive on being successful on defense and in those first eight minutes of the game, the Oilers were as good as any team in the nation.

"Our intensity in the first seven, eight minutes of the game was the difference," Niekamp said, as he sat in his office after the game glancing at the box score. "It was pretty even after that. I thought we had stretches of excellence on defense and that is a good sign."

Five games were on the books and all five had been played in the friendly confines of Croy

Gymnasium. The Oilers now had to take their act on the road for a showdown with Grand Valley. Nine months after the miserable March night in the NCAA tournament, the Oilers were going to get their first shot at revenge.

14 REVENGE - PART 1

Time is supposed to heal all wounds but nine months later, the scar from the NCAA tourney loss to Grand Valley State was still visible. No matter how hard Findlay tried, it couldn't forget all that went wrong that night. The other two losses the Oilers suffered last season hurt, as well.

"We have those losses in the back of our minds," Lewis said, after a practice the week of the game. "We remember what it felt like afterwards, especially the last one. I remember walking off the floor each time saying we wouldn't lose the next time. It didn't work out but we want to go up this week and make a statement."

Parker, confident as always, echoed those thoughts.

"We still remember what it was like to lose to them but it's a different story this year," Parker, said during an interview. "We are motivated and we understand our roles. If we play our roles, everything else will take care of itself."

The Lakers were 6-1 and ranked No. 11 in the nation, which meant the game was going to carry weight for not only the conference standings but for the NCAA regional rankings that would be released in January. Grand Valley, which no longer had Eziukwu or Jamerson, had just been beaten 68-67 by Ashland University on the road. Even if the Lakers looked a bit vulnerable, the Oilers could not afford to take them lightly.

"They are still working on gelling as a team," Niekamp said, in an interview after practice. "They have a talented team, though, and whenever we play each other, there is great intensity on both sides."

Sophomore guard/forward, Justin Ringler, was the top scoring threat for the Lakers, averaging 13 points per game, while Trammell, now a senior, was clicking for 12.4 points per outing. The Lakers averaged 73 points per game as a team and gave up 61.3. As the Oilers, the Lakers took a lot of pride in playing hard on defense. Establishing breathing room in the showdown was not going to be easy for either team. Bostic would have to continue his solid play for the Oilers to have a chance against the Lakers. Through five games, he had lived up to the hype, averaging 18 points and 6.6 rebounds per game. Four other Oilers were averaging at least 10 points.

"We continue to make strides," Niekamp said. "Our guys have experience to draw on and they know the key to winning a championship is finding road wins."

Nine months of waiting were about to come to an end. It was time for the Oilers to take a swing at revenge and hope they could land the knockout punch.

"We want to play our butts off," Lewis said. "We know they're ranked but we're ranked, too. We're going to be ready to play."

As expected, the game was tight. The Oilers clung to a 20-16 lead with four minutes remaining in the opening half on the afternoon of Dec. 13 in Allendale. Two straight 3-pointers off the hot hand of Evans stretched the Findlay lead to 26-16. Bostic answered moments later with a trey of his own after coming up with a steal and the Oilers surged into halftime with a 33-18 advantage. Grand Valley's usually raucous crowd was silenced. They Oilers smelled blood in the water as they headed to the locker room. Evans talked about why the Oilers were so successful getting open for outside shots against a defense that doesn't give up many easy opportunities.

"They switched over to a zone and we hit some 3's," Evans said. "Nate hit a couple of 3-pointers, I hit a couple and Josh hit one. I just think they got confused. We were beating them from inside and outside."

Although no lead is ever safe, especially on the road, the Oilers had no intentions of letting the Lakers back into the game. Hyde got the second half rolling with a 3-pointer and ended his day with 13 points. Parker and Bostic scored 12 points apiece. Bostic also grabbed seven rebounds and dished out five assists, the latest example of Bostic's ability to be an all-around great player. Roberts finished with seven points and seven rebounds. The Oilers shot 46.8 percent from the field and held the Lakers to only four field goals in the second half as they pulled away for a 68-47 win.

"It's easy to get tentative with a lead when you are on the road," Niekamp said. "I thought we showed a lot of poise. We didn't rush things. We made extra passes and took our time to get good shots."

After the game, I noticed Bostic standing in front of the Grand Valley trophy case. His attention was captured by the picture inside of it. It was a picture of the Sweet 16 game the Oilers played in March and it brought back the feeling of pain from that night yet Bostic could smile, knowing a much better memory had just been made.

Not only did the Oilers beat the Lakers, they also ended the Lakers' thirty-eight-game home win streak.

"Looking at that picture brought back dreadful memories but everything feels good right now," Bostic said. "It's our first time winning on this floor since I've been here. It's a credit to our coaches and our team."

Much of the success is a credit to the defense the Oilers played against the Lakers. They forced twenty-one turnovers and scored 24 points off those miscues.

"The old saying is defense creates offense," Bostic said. "Playing good defense made up for the shots we missed. Our game plan was to come here and play great defense. I believe we did that."

Now it was time for the Oilers to head out of the arena and travel an hour North on US Highway 31 to Big Rapids. A rare Sunday afternoon game was up next for the Oilers as they would battle Ferris State at Jim Wink Arena to finish off a two-game road swing in Michigan.

15 BULLDOG BUSTERS

I checked out of my hotel on the morning of December 14th and headed up the snow-lined highway to Big Rapids to cover the game against Ferris State. It was going to take a heck of an effort by the Oilers to cap this trip with a second consecutive win. Ferris State had won just three of its first seven and Justin Keenan was their go-to-guy and one of the rising stars in the GLIAC. He was averaging 21 points per game. Like the fieldhouse at Grand Valley, Jim Wink Arena was a tough place to play. The fans are passionate and can get loud in a hurry if things start falling apart for the opposing team. The last two games the Oilers and Bulldogs played against each other in the building had been decided by 5 points or less.

Ferris State opted to come out playing a zone defense, hoping to disrupt the shooting rhythm of the Oilers. It was a horrible idea. Findlay hit jumpers and 3-pointers with relative ease in the opening half, connecting six times from beyond the arc and shooting nearly 60 percent from the floor in the first twenty minutes. The hot touch helped fuel an 18-0 run that all but broke the will of the Bulldogs. Lewis nailed a jumper in the lane to ignite the run and Bostic finished the offensive outburst with his third 3-pointer of the game. Hyde drilled two treys in the first half and the Oilers rolled into halftime with a 42-29 advantage.

"They started off in a zone and let us shoot the ball," said Roberts, who was a little surprised the Bulldogs were daring enough to use the zone. "They learned the hard way we can shoot."

Ferris State head coach Bill Sall, one of the more animated coaches in the conference— he typically threw off his suit jacket as soon as the intensity of the game rose to a certain level or, if he became frustrated with calls by the officials, figured his defensive game plan would be effective. What he saw that Sunday afternoon was a far cry from what he saw on film from a Findlay team that came in shooting close to 50 percent from the field.

"We went zone because, based on the tapes we saw, we thought they looked iffy shooting the ball," Sall said. "It was tough falling behind so quickly. It's a lesson learned for us."

The Oilers refused to let up in the second half and nailed down an 83-60 win. Findlay showed no signs of the wear and tear that comes with playing on the road. The Oilers played with intensity the Bulldogs could not match and forced them into eighteen turnovers, turning those miscues into 28 points. They also held a 32-25 edge on the boards, thanks in large part to the play of Roberts, who grabbed eleven rebounds to go along with his 10 points.

"I think it's annoying how we play defense," Lewis said after the game. "We are always in their face. We are rotating and screaming to let each other know where people are. It's frustrating for people to handle."

Bostic paced the Oilers with 18 points. Hyde came through with 11 points. Keenan scored 16 points to lead the Bulldogs but got little help from his teammates. No one else from Ferris State scored more than 9. Niekamp was impressed his team was able to nail down a convincing road win after it poured so much into beating Grand Valley less than twenty-four hours earlier.

"After the effort we put into Saturday's game and to come back and play on short notice, our guys deserve a lot of credit," Niekamp said, in the hallway outside the Findlay locker room. "We were able to get two good wins over two good teams."

The Oilers were now 7-0 overall and 4-0 in the conference and, on this day, I started to realize how special this Findlay team was shaping up to be. The players were loose and wearing big smiles in the locker room, joking around with each other as they savored their latest win. You could see the players embraced the life of being the No. 1 team in the nation.

So much more basketball was still left to be played as the Oilers packed their bags late Sunday afternoon and boarded their charter bus for the ride home. Being able to sweep this trip provided a jolt of confidence for the Oilers and it served as a reminder to the rest of the Division II basketball world that this team, and this season, was unfolding in a way that would be unlike any other in the history of the program.

16 CHARGED UP WHILE BEING NO. 1

It can be overwhelming to be the best but, unlike other great teams playing with the ultimate bullseye on their backs, Findlay refused to succumb to the pressure.

"When we walked into the gym, the crowd could sense that we had a certain swag to us that couldn't be touched," Lewis recalled, a few years after the championship season. "We knew if we went out and executed what we had been going over in practice and in film sessions, the team we played wouldn't be able to stop us."

Even Bostic said the Oilers went out and expected to win. They believed they were the best team in the gym, although that didn't mean they weren't going to have to work hard to earn the win. They were as confident as any team in the country and confidence was starting to shine through, even more after two big road wins.

"We expected to be successful, but we also know every game is a dogfight," Bostic said. "The big thing

81

for us is anyone on this team can come out and have a big night. There isn't one person you can focus on. It's important to our success."

Every player bought into the system and every player believed they were good enough to be champions as long as they continued to play up to their potential and remain focused.

"The coaching staff did an excellent job of taking it one game at a time," Lewis said. "We didn't care we were undefeated. We wanted to win the next game we played. We wanted to go out every time and prove we were the best team in the country."

Making that statement night after night wouldn't be easy. The Oilers still had a lot of basketball left in their season. Despite the challenges ahead, Niekamp made sure his team took time to savor each moment.

"The conference schedule is a long haul, and we have a long, tough road ahead," Niekamp said in an interview after the win over Ferris State. "There will be ups and downs. The best thing to do is to appreciate every win you get, whether it's at home or on the road, and then move on to the next one."

What became clear as Findlay prepared to battle Hillsdale Dec. 18 at Jesse Phillips Arena was the Oilers understood the importance of teamwork. Bostic, the best player in the country, was Findlay's top scoring threat, averaging just over 17 points per game through seven games. Four other players were averaging at least nine points. Ten players had seen action in at least six games and eight were averaging ten or more minutes per game.

"If a starter isn't having a good game, we can depend on someone else to lead the way, whether it's another starter or someone off the bench," Bostic said. "It's a credit to the program coach Niekamp has built here."

The benefit of using a system where one player isn't counted on to be the star paid off in a variety of ways. The impact foul trouble had on the Oilers was minimized and injuries were a little easier to overcome. Ernst also noted the experience players gained early in their careers prepared them to step into more prominent roles down the road.

"We recruit mostly high school kids and they buy into their roles and wait their turn, and when they get it, they are ready," Ernst said in an interview. "Rarely is the offensive success here based around one or two players. Ron instills the attitude of sharing the ball and taking good shots."

In the win over Ferris State, the Oilers put their teamwork on display. The starters combined to take only 31 shots and the Oilers finished with fifteen assists as a team.

"Look at Findlay. They are very good at sharing the ball," Sall said, after his Bulldogs lost to the Oilers. "They have an All-American (Bostic) and he only takes nine shots. There isn't one guy you can focus on."

It was Hillsdale's turn to deal with the balance of the Oilers and, if history was any indication, things weren't expected to go well for the Chargers, who trailed 33-5 in the all-time series. Still, Hillsdale is always tough to deal with. The Chargers play hard and play smart. They entered the game at 5-1 overall and 3-0 in the GLIAC, averaging 72.5 points per game and giving up 68.7. The Oilers, who had allowed 60 points only once all season, were prepared to match the intensity of the Chargers in this crucial showdown on the road.

"We're excited about playing Hillsdale and we expect them to bring their best effort," said Lewis, who was averaging 11.1 points per game and had tallied twenty-one steals. "But we are gunning for everyone and we are going to play our best, too. We want to prove every night why we are who we are."

The trip to Hillsdale was an easy one, barely two hours from home. My seat for the game was in a press box high above the gym floor, which provided a good view of the action for a game pitting the only two teams with perfect records in conference play. It didn't take long for the Oilers to send a message. Hyde knocked down a 3-pointer to start off the game and the Oilers would hit on their first four attempts from long range as they crippled the Chargers with a 22-3 run. Evans capped the outburst with a trey and the Oilers rumbled into halftime with a 40-21 advantage. They would go on to win 70-56.

"That run was just what the doctor ordered since this was our third road game in a row," Niekamp said in a post-game interview. "We really came out with a lot of enthusiasm, shot the ball well and did a good job of playing defense. We put them in a tough position and that is what you want to do against a team on the road."

The Oilers were on top of their game from a shooting standpoint, connecting at a 49 percent clip from the field and Bostic and Lewis teamed up to make life miserable for the Chargers. Bostic dropped in 18 points and grabbed ten rebounds, marking his second double-double of the season. Lewis torched the Chargers for 17 points and pulled down eleven rebounds. The scoring effort by Bostic pushed him into thirtieth all-time on the school scoring list with 1,175 points. Anthony Slappy, who played at Findlay from 1987 until 1990, was previously at No. 30 with 1,164 points. Niekamp wasn't surprised by the performances of his two stars.

"They are veteran players and you rely on them to have good games," Niekamp said. "They gave us a great effort, first on defense then with their rebounding and scoring."

Hyde scored 10 points and Roberts and Parker finished with 8 points apiece. The Chargers were unable to match the effort. Tony Gugino, a 6-foot-9 senior preseason All-GLIAC selection, did his part for Hillsdale by scoring 21 points. No one else provided any help as the Chargers shot only 38 percent from the field and were ice cold from beyond the arc, hitting only two of their twenty attempts.

"I don't think they were so much desperation 3-pointers as they were shots taken out of rhythm," Niekamp said. "They were not in a comfort zone shooting the ball."

Hillsdale never got closer than 13 points in the second half and gave up 18 points off thirteen turnovers. Findlay now had an eleven-day Christmas break before returning to action Dec. 29 for a non-conference game against Wisconsin-Parkside in Kenosha.

"We'll give the guys four or five days to spend time with their families for Christmas before we get ready for our trip to Wisconsin," Niekamp said. "We feel good about this win, though. It's a great road win over a very talented Hillsdale team."

The Oilers headed into the break at 8-0 overall and 5-0 in the conference. They felt good about their latest win and planned to enjoy their well-deserved break before getting back to their pursuit of greatness.

17 ROAD TEST IN WISCONSIN

If there was ever a game where the Oilers were prone to an upset it was on the final Monday night of 2008 against Parkside at DiSimone Gymnasium in Kenosha. Parkside, a GLVC team, came into the contest battle-tested, having already faced two nationally ranked opponents. The Rangers lost both of those games and were only 3-6. Findlay needed to steal the momentum early against the Rangers and it did, opening the game on a 19-7 run. Findlay looked anything but rusty from the break as it rattled the confidence of the Rangers.

"You are always concerned when you're coming off a break but I thought we had a good approach to the game," Niekamp said. "We got off to a great start."

Findlay rolled into halftime with a 47-28 lead but the thing about Parkside is that it didn't know the meaning of quit. Earlier in the season, the Rangers trailed Indiana-Northwest by 27 points with 11:30 remaining in the game before roaring back for a 91-88 win. Lavontay Fenderson scored 44 points in the comeback and he was in a groove against the Oilers as well as he helped trigger a rally. The Rangers closed their deficit to 14 points several times. The Oilers were able to shoot well enough from the free-throw line and play at a high level on the defensive end of the floor to secure an 88-74 win. Findlay shot 16-of-17 from the line, including a 10-of-11 effort from Bostic and, also, forced seventeen turnovers. The Oilers shot a sizzling 63.5 percent from the field overall, including at a 68 percent clip in the first half and Parkside shot 44.6 percent from the floor in the loss. Fenderson dropped in 32 points, the most any player had scored against the Oilers all season and the Rangers were also the first team of the season to score more than 70 points against the Oilers, who came in allowing just 57 points per game—the ninth-best average in the nation.

"I give a lot of credit to Fenderson. He is a tremendous player and was a tough matchup for us," Niekamp said. "He played hard. He wasn't going to let his team just roll over."

For the second straight game, Bostic and Lewis took charge. Bostic hung 24 points on the Rangers. Lewis lit up the scoreboard for 22. Parker and Roberts rose to the occasion as well, chipping in 12 and 10 points, respectively.

"You expect your veterans to play well and they came ready for a forty-minute battle tonight," Niekamp said. "I thought we shot very well from the free-throw line and that shows our players were tuned in and focused."

Speaking of veterans, the game provided Laflin with a chance to play again. He had missed the first seven games, while recovering from a broken ankle and played three minutes against Parkside. It was a small step forward for a player the Oilers needed as the season rolled on. The win over Parkside also carried importance because it was an in-region game. The victory on the road would prove to be a feather in the cap of the Oilers in their quest to host the NCAA regional in March.

"We talked to the team about how games against regional opponents have added distinction," Niekamp said. "This was an important win for us."

Just like that, two months of the season were history. The Oilers started the season with insanely high expectations and had done a remarkable job of living up to them, especially when one considers Findlay's final four games of December were played on the road. The calendar was about to flip to 2009 and the Oilers prepared to head into the brutal grind of their regular-season schedule. Not only would the Oilers be battling for a conference championship but their NCAA tournament fate also hinged on how well they played in the next two months.

18 AVOIDING SHOCK

Findlay was scheduled to play Hillsdale for the second time on Jan. 3. It would be the final meeting of the regular season between the two South Division rivals, with the Oilers gunning for the sweep of the season series. Earlier in the week, I was able to able catch up with Hyde to talk about his season and get his thoughts on round two with the Chargers. Hyde had been a starter since the fourth game of the season and excelled in the role, averaging 11 points per game and emerging as one of the top 3-point shooting threats in the country, drilling a team-best twenty-three treys. He had scored in double figures in seven of the Oilers' first nine games.

"My teammates have done a good job of getting me the ball and I've been fortunate to make shots," said Hyde, who mentioned he worked hard in the offseason on developing a quicker release to his shot. "I'm playing with a lot of confidence and doing what I can to help the team."

Hyde was coming off a 3-of-6 showing from 3-

point range in the win over the Rangers, and his 3-point percentage on the year was the 20th-best in the country. I remember covering a Liberty Benton game a few years earlier when Hyde was a junior in high school. Hyde was being recruited by Findlay at the time but a couple of people told me they questioned if he could play at the D-II level. I knew Hyde was more than good enough to do it and he did a good job of silencing any doubters. Hyde provided glimpses of his phenomenal potential during the opening round of the NCAA tournament his freshman season. The Oilers took on Lewis and Hyde looked nothing like a freshman playing in the sometimes blinding spotlight of the NCAA tourney. Hyde wasn't consumed by the moment, drilling three treys during a second-half rally that helped catapult Findlay to a 64-57 win. The performance served as a huge boost to his growth as a player.

"Anytime you can play in a situation like that and have success, you're going to learn not to be afraid to take shots," Hyde said. "It was a big help to play well in that game."

It wasn't just the NCAA tournament experience that proved beneficial to Hyde. The fact that he could turn to Evans for advice also played a role in his success. "He has taught me a lot about reading defenses and getting in a position to take good shots," Hyde said. "It's nice to be able to get advice from him."

Hillsdale was coming to town in the grip of a 3-game losing streak. The Chargers, sitting at 5-4 overall and 3-2 in the GLIAC, lost all three games during the slide to nationally ranked opponents, including one to the Oilers in December. Gugino was still the go-to guy for the Chargers, averaging 15.6 points and 8.0 rebounds per game. Although the Oilers had beaten them once, it was no guarantee for success a second time.

"They have a very talented group of players and they are capable of shooting the ball very well," Niekamp said, in a phone interview earlier in the week. "We had a good game against them the last time we played but they will come ready to play."

Ready might have been an understatement. The Chargers came out of the gate energized, stunning the sold-out crowd inside Croy Gymnasium by building a 21-6 advantage with ten minutes left in the opening half. Hillsdale attacked the basket at will for easy layups and made it extremely difficult for the Oilers to get good looks. As the half wore on, it looked as if the Chargers were positioning themselves for one of their biggest wins in program history and hand the Oilers a rare home loss. The majority of the time, an opponent was lucky to have a lead of any kind in Croy. For the Chargers to have the Oilers in a 15-point hole, well, it was surprising.

"It was shocking, especially at home," Roberts said. "I can't remember us ever being down like that here."

Bostic wasn't going to stand by and let the Chargers ruin the Oilers' run at perfection. With Hillsdale point guard Tyler Gerber dribbling the ball up the floor, Bostic hounded him and forced him to give up the ball. Bostic raced the other way and soared into the lane for a one-hand dunk that whipped the fans into a frenzy and trimmed the Hillsdale lead to 21-14.

"Defense wins championships," Bostic said. "We knew we had to pick up our intensity if we were going to get back in the game."

The play injected a shot of life into the Oilers, who closed the gap to 23-20 with a few minutes remaining in the first half. Good shots became tougher to come by for the Chargers and Hyde and Laflin both connected on 3-pointers during the furious run to knock the Chargers back on their heels. As the final seconds ticked off the clock in the first half, the Oilers staring up at a 30-27 deficit, Sparks came through with a big-time play. He launched up an off-balance 3-point shot that sliced through the net as time expired. The score was tied at 30-30; or so the Oilers thought. The basket was initially waved off because the clock at one end of the gym showed no time remaining when Sparks released the ball. The clock on the other scoreboard had two-tenths of life left on it. The officials met for a short discussion and ruled the basket was good. The feeling I got as Findlay headed to the locker room was the Chargers were about to pay dearly for tugging on Superman's cape early in the game.

"The shot gave us momentum," Niekamp said. "I think our players felt like they had gotten off the hook after a tough start. Those first ten minutes were ugly. Hillsdale deserves credit for that."

Hillsdale was helpless in the second half. Bostic drove into the lane and scored on a layup as he drew a foul. His ensuing free throw gave the Oilers their first lead at 33-30. The play was the start of a 19-4 run that would leave the Chargers wondering what happened. By the time the run was finished on a layup by Roberts, the Oilers held a 49-34 lead. The

Chargers were never the same and scored only 18 points in the second half as the Oilers rolled to a 71-48 win to improve to 10-0 overall and to 6-0 in the GLIAC.

"Hillsdale has a great team and it says a lot about our defense that we were able to hold them down like we did," said Bostic, who scored only seven points but was rock solid on defense as he tallied six steals.

What the Oilers did to the Chargers in the second half was impressive. Their defensive performance offered a glimpse of just how good they could be when they locked down on defense. Roberts paced the Oilers with 15 points and six rebounds. Lewis scored 12 points. Laflin took another step forward in his recovery, seeing a major amount of time as Parker was limited to fourteen minutes because of foul trouble. Laflin capitalized on the extended playing time as he scored 8 points and grabbed three rebounds. Niekamp was thrilled about his team's effort. He also noted Findlay was a long way away from reaching its full potential.

"We gave a good effort once we started playing better," Niekamp said. "I think part of our problem early was that we had already beaten them once easily and so, maybe, we were expecting an easy game. There are no automatic wins in the GLIAC. We learned that we have not arrived as a team yet."

19 MOTOR CITY MAGIC

One of their toughest games of the season awaited the Oilers as they entered the first full week of January. Findlay had to play Wayne State on Jan. 5 in Detroit. The Warriors have a reputation for being one of the hardest-working teams in the GLIAC. Everyone knew veteran head coach David Greer would have his team ready to go for this Thursday night showdown. The early part of the season had been a struggle for the Warriors, who were 4-6 overall and 2-4 in the conference. They had lost five of their last six games and were led by a pair of transfers, including Shane Lawal from Division I Oakland University. Lawal was averaging 14.2 points per outing and also grabbing a team-best 9.3 rebounds per game. The 6-foot-9 redshirt senior center had also blocked thirty-nine shots. Junior guard Bryan Wright out of Lakeland Community College was the leading scorer, averaging 15.1 points per game. Lawal and Wright were two of the eight newcomers the Warriors had on their roster.

"They have a lot of new players and so we don't know much about them other than what we've seen on tape," Niekamp said, in an interview after practice earlier in the week. "Greer always has his team ready to play. We will have to work hard to get another GLIAC road win."

Wayne State had not beaten the Oilers since Valentine's Day in 2005, when Findlay came to the Motor City ranked No. 2 in the country. The Oilers were going to need a stellar effort to get out of Detroit with a win. Laflin would have to be one of the players who would need to step up, especially because the play of a team's bench is key to success on the road. Laflin had slowly worked himself back into a groove in his first two games after the injury, and reflected on the challenge of missing the first eight games of the season. "It wasn't fun being on the bench," Laflin said. "It feels great to finally be back. Getting back to where I was before the injury isn't going to happen overnight. I feel good and I know when I come in, I'm going to play hard and bring energy to the team."

Energy wasn't in short supply for the Oilers as the action got underway inside the Matthei Building in downtown Detroit. Findlay blitzed Wayne State out of the gate, opening the game on a 15-3 run. Bostic led the way as he scored 19 points in the first half and helped push UF into halftime with a 48-30 advantage. It didn't faze the Oilers at all that they were playing their fifth road game since Dec. 13. They played with confidence and made smart decisions. Still, Wayne State refused to fold. Findlay came up empty on its shot attempts in the first six minutes of the second half as the Warriors tightened up on defense and cut the UF lead to 63-57 with less than ten minutes to play. Bryan Smothers helped fuel the comeback on a night when he hit all five of his attempts from beyond the arc enroute to scoring 24 points.

Bostic answered as one would expect a National Player of the Year candidate to do in a game where momentum was slipping away in a hurry. He lined up for a 3-pointer in the corner and swished it through, helping the Oilers get back on track. The shot ignited a 23-7 run, putting the game out of reach. Bostic was unreal as he torched the Warriors for a career-high 31 points. He hit 10-of-19 shots from the field and knocked down four 3-pointers as he moved into 24th all-time in scoring with 1,237 points. I joked with Bostic after the 92-77 win that his performance was almost Michael Jordan-like. He laughed at the comparison.

"Sometimes you have nights like that," said Bostic, whose previous career-high was 29. "My success is a credit to my teammates. They gave me opportunities and I took advantage."

Parker delivered a sensational performance as well, going off for 20 points and dishing out four assists. He also racked up five steals and turned the ball over only twice. Roberts nearly had a double-double as he scored 8 points and grabbed ten rebounds. He also played a pivotal role in containing Lawal, who managed only 8 points and seven rebounds.

"Lee did a great job on Shane," Niekamp said. "He made him work for everything he got."

Lewis stepped up as well, scoring 11 points, and the Oilers shot 50 percent from the field, as a team, to ring up their twenty-third consecutive win in the regular season. Findlay also forced eighteen turnovers and converted them into 27 points.

"I can tell you there are plenty of other teams I would rather have played tonight than Findlay," Greer said, in an interview outside his team's locker room. We competed hard and fought back but we were not ready to play a team like Findlay."

This game could have gone easily the other way had the Warriors been at their best. The Oilers, though, understood the importance of executing on both ends of the floor and being prepared to play at a high level on the road.

"Every road win in this conference is so important," Niekamp said. "The veteran players understand that. This is not an easy place to play but I thought we handled it quite well."

As usual, there would be little time for the Oilers to enjoy their latest accomplishment as their next challenge was a game against Northwood on Saturday in Midland, Mich. The Oilers, at 11-0 overall and 7-0 in the conference, were going to have to dig deep to grind out a win over the Timberwolves, less than forty-eight hours after battling the Warriors.

20 KNOCKING DOWN NORTHWOOD

The second game of a two-game road swing in the GLIAC is always the toughest. Sure, the road team has an off day to rest and prepare for the next game but travel wears on a team. The shots don't go down as easily, it's tougher to defend and mistakes are magnified. Northwood had gotten off to a strong start, fashioning a 9-3 overall record and a 5-2 mark in the conference. The Timberwolves, as is the case with most teams in the North Division of the GLIAC, love to play a physical and bruising brand of basketball. That style of play kept the Timberwolves in the game early against the Oilers. They challenged Findlay in the paint and shot well from the field to stay within striking distance of an upset victory. Had it not been for a 3-pointer at the buzzer by Hyde, Findlay would have only gone into halftime with a two-point lead, instead of a 30-25 advantage.

Although the score was a little too close for comfort, the Oilers had become good at putting together a back-breaking run that would all but wipe out the victory hopes of an opposing team. Roberts, saddled with foul trouble in the first half, which forced him to spend most of the half on the bench, appeared to have the Oilers headed in the right direction when he scored six straight points to put Findlay in front 36-30. His two free throws during the stretch lit the fire for a 20-2 run that ended with Hyde drilling a 3-pointer, giving the Oilers a 53-32 lead. Game, set, match—or so it seemed.

Marcus Moore, who scored 15 points and Mark Barnes, who finished with 11 points, refused to let the Timberwolves get blown out at home. Moore came through with a clutch 3-pointer that cut the Findlay lead to 58-47. Moore's trey, with under a minute to play, trimmed the Oilers' lead to 72-69. Findlay was on the brink of stumbling for the first time. To make matters worse, Bostic fouled out while Lewis and Roberts were both in foul trouble. If the Oilers were going to stay perfect, someone else had to step up. In the final eighteen seconds, Hyde found himself in the role of go-to-guy for the Oilers. He was fouled three times in the closing seconds and went to the free-throw line each time. A miss or two on any of those free throw attempts would be costly. But Hyde delivered in crunch time, drilling all six of his free throws as the Oilers held on for a 78-71 victory and improved to 12-0. Those free throws were his only shots from the line on the day but Hyde did hit three shots from beyond the arc and was six-of-eleven overall from the field, as he finished with a career-high 21 points.

"It was a big plus to hit those free throws late in the game," Niekamp said. "Nate's six free throws at the end were big and you need players to do that in close games."

The Timberwolves shot a sizzling 57.8 percent from the field but part of the reason the Oilers were able to hang on was because Wilhite and Wehri provided valuable play off the bench. Wilhite scored seven points and grabbed four rebounds in twelve minutes of work. Wehri also played twelve minutes and set several screens to set up open looks for Findlay's outside shooters. Wehri also grabbed three rebounds.

"Antoine and Jason both did a nice job off the bench," Niekamp said. "We had some careless fouls today but we fought through it."

The Oilers shot 41.5 percent from the field but were 27-of-34 from the free-throw line. Bostic finished with 12 points and Parker scored 10 points. As for Hyde's effort, Niekamp was impressed.

"They were giving Nate good looks at the basket," Niekamp said. "It was good to see him step up the way he did."

For the Oilers to come out of the week with two wins was huge—not to mention the challenges the Oilers faced on the trip, especially against Northwood, which would serve them well as they continued their journey.

21 WAXING THE WILDCATS

Preparing to play Findlay is never easy. For opposing coaches, it's all about deciding how to defend the Oilers' best players, while worrying about which role players are going to step up. It's a process that can keep coaches up late and add a little gray to their hair. Findlay was scheduled to play Northern Michigan on Jan. 15 and battle Michigan Tech two days later. Both games were at home. I decided to get in touch with the coaches of Northern and Tech via telephone to talk about what goes into getting ready for a game against Findlay. I talked with Northern Michigan head coach Dean Ellis first and he offered his insight into the challenges of getting ready for the Oilers.

"Ron obviously has a deep and talented team," Ellis said. "He does an outstanding job in creating preparation issues for teams by implementing a number of defenses and offensive sets to his game plan. The diversity forces all of us to spend additional time in preparing our players and game plan."

Michigan Tech head coach Kevin Luke, one of the

most personable coaches around and, perhaps, the most well-liked opposing coach in the conference, said the Oilers are viewed as a measuring stick. Luke has had his share of success against the Oilers over the years and even led the Huskies to league tournament championships in 2002 and 2003. Facing Findlay, however, presented a different kind of challenge.

"Findlay is by far the best team in the league and I think you have to set realistic goals against them," Luke said. "Playing Findlay is everyone's opportunity to see how they measure up against the best. Opponents have to play at the highest possible level to beat them. We are looking forward to the challenge."

Niekamp has never been a coach to put all of the pressure on one player to lead the way. Sure, the Oilers had Bostic and he was hands down the best player in the nation but it didn't mean he had to be the star night every night. Through twelve games, the Oilers had five players averaging 10 or more points, including Bostic, who was averaging 17.7 points per game and they were giving up only 60.5 points per outing, the tenth-best average in the country. Lewis was averaging 12.3 points per outing. Hyde was scoring 11.6 points per game and Roberts was at 10.6 points per game. Parker was coming through with an average of 10.3 points per outing.

"We have so many guys that can hurt you offensively," Niekamp said. "We can play a lot of guys, too, and that allows our starters to rest. On defense, everyone plays hard and we continue to make strides in that area."

Northern Michigan was coming to town at 9-4

overall and 4-4 in the GLIAC. Marc Renelique was the Wildcats' biggest star, averaging 16.9 points per outing and had just been named the GLIAC North Division Player of the Week after torching Ashland University for 32 points in an 84-76 loss. Senior forward Raymont McElroy was averaging 10.8 points per game and had also racked up 35 assists and 17 steals. Northern Michigan wasn't bad on defense as it was allowing only 62.6 points per game. It was shooting 44.3 percent from the field and nearly 40 percent (38.2) from 3-point range.

"They aren't as physical as they have been in past years," Niekamp said. "They are more perimeter-oriented and have shot the ball well. They will play a lot of 2-3 zone against us defensively."

Tech was led by Robby Springborn, a senior guard who was averaging 13.9 points per game. He had dished out thirty-one assists and tallied seventeen steals, as well. The Huskies, sitting at 8-5 overall and 5-3 in the GLIAC, were the best defensive team in the league in terms of points allowed as they gave up 55.9 per game. It was going to be interesting to see how the Oilers handled the Huskies as Findlay was clearly the league's most dangerous offensive team. First, Findlay had to worry about the Wildcats. This Findlay team had done a tremendous job of not looking ahead and it wasn't about to veer off that path.

Game time arrived and the Oilers were as ready as they could be for the Wildcats' visit to Croy Gymnasium. Prayer seemed to be the only option for Northern Michigan on this night. The Wildcats were forced to take shots with a defender in their face every time, drives into the lane came up empty and, on the flip side, they had no luck slowing down the determined Oilers. Northern Michigan scored only 8 points in the first twelve minutes, shot only 16.1 percent from the field in the first half and found the rim just once on thirteen attempts from beyond the arc. Findlay was on another level, drilling shots from the outside, attacking the Wildcats with a steady diet of dunks, including a couple by Lewis, and easy layups were set up by making the extra pass. The Oilers' near-perfect execution translated into a 47-12 lead at halftime.

"Giving up 12 points in the first half is a great accomplishment," Sparks said. "We are a great defensive team and we need to play like we did tonight every night."

Sparks shined in the win, scoring a career-high 19 points, hitting all six of his shots from the field, including a 3-for-3 effort from 3-point range, and he also made all four of his free throws. Sparks pulled down five rebounds as well. For Sparks, who prides himself on being a physical defender, his breakout game on offense was a great sign. Of course, Niekamp was able to find a minor flaw in Sparks' performance on a night when the Oilers blasted the Wildcats 96-47 to push their record to 13-0 overall and to 9-0 in the GLIAC.

"Tyler did have one turnover," Niekamp said, with a laugh in a post-game interview. "He is maturing as a player. He is a physical kid and tonight he got his offensive game going. He is a dangerous player when he does that."

The Oilers shot 55.7 percent from the field and connected on eleven of their twenty-four attempts from beyond the arc. They forced fifteen turnovers, including ten in the first half, and held the Wildcats to 26.2 percent shooting from the field. Renelique, so important to Northern Michigan's success, managed to score only 11 points. Those 11 points were the most by any Wildcat in the game. Sparks was pleased that he was able to play a key role in the win, although he was quick to deflect credit to his teammates.

"It was a great game by the whole team," Sparks said. "Everyone scored tonight. That says something about our team."

Bostic lit up the scoreboard for 17 points, pushing his career total to 1,266 (23rd all-time), and he also dished out five assists. Roberts came through with 15 points and six rebounds. Parker added nine points. Niekamp knew the Wildcats' long trip to Ohio had something to do with their struggles. He also gave a ton of credit to his own team.

"It shows the effect travel can have on a team because Northern is a lot better than it showed tonight," Niekamp said. "But our guys deserve credit. We made it difficult for them to run their offense. When you play aggressive on defense, good things happen."

22 DOMINATING THE HUSKIES

The fact that Findlay was coming off a convincing win on Thursday night meant the odds were much higher for a letdown in the next game. It happens all of the time in college basketball. A team rolls over one opponent and then lacks the energy and intensity it needs to do the same in the next game. The Huskies were always ready to play, although on this day in Croy Gymnasium, they weren't ready for the level Findlay would play at in this rivalry game.

Roberts sparked the Oilers early as he blocked a couple of shots, helping to set the tone with defense, and Hyde drilled two 3-pointers as Findlay knocked Tech back on its heels in the opening minutes of the game, building a commanding 16-0 lead. The crowd roared as Luke burned a timeout in the hopes of slowing down the Oilers' momentum. It didn't help.

"We were concerned with how prepared we would be after playing (Thursday)," Niekamp said. "We forced turnovers. The start was vital to the game."

Tech battled back and trimmed the Findlay lead to

22-13 with nine minutes remaining, thanks to the play of Sean Geary, who scored 17 points. Findlay led 44-26 at halftime and shot 52.8 percent from the field as it rolled to an 83-69 win. Luke has the utmost respect for the Oilers, and he talked about his concerns with playing Findlay earlier in the week. His Huskies never stopped playing hard. It's not their style to give up. Findlay was simply the better team.

"They have no weak option, not even on the bench," Luke said. "You can't play normal defense against them because they have so many weapons."

Hyde is one of those weapons, and he had his shooting touch working for him against Tech. He hit on all four of his attempts from beyond the arc and scored 16 points. Lewis chimed in with 13 points and Parker scored 12 to go along with five assists. Roberts, so full of energy and such a dominating force in the post, scored 11 points and grabbed nine rebounds as he nearly finished with a double-double. The senior center made one mistake, at least according to Bostic, who finished with eight points but made an impact in other ways as he grabbed seven rebounds and dished out five assists. As I was getting ready to talk with Roberts outside the locker room, Bostic came out and started bouncing a ball off the wall. He joked that Roberts should start practicing his passing and catching a little more; both players laughed. The moment offered a glimpse of how loose this team was and how much it was enjoying life as the nation's top team. The Oilers were now 14-0 overall and 10-0 in the conference. Roberts talked about his strong play early in the game and the energy he once again brought to the gym as the Oilers took care of business one more time.

"I like coming out and starting games with a lot of energy," Roberts said. "I had a couple of good blocks that got the momentum going and we were able to build a big lead."

The Oilers did a lot of their damage with defense, forcing seventeen turnovers, and turning those miscues into 26 points. The Huskies had two other players in double figures besides Geary; Springborn scored 13 points and Don Fowler added 11, they shot 41 percent from the field as a team. One of the difference makers against the Huskies was Parker, who was great at breaking down defenses and finding the open man. His play at the point guard position was instrumental in Findlay's unbeaten start and his effort against Tech helped the Oilers earn another win.

"Marcus is doing a good job of distributing the ball, finding the right guy at the right time," Niekamp said. "Nate made everything he looked at and Evans came off the bench and hit two big 3's. Our efficiency on offense is getting better."

Of course, the Oilers never walked away from a game completely satisfied and that approach was a big part of why they had reached the midway point of the regular season with a perfect record. They understood no team was going to make life easy for them and that any let up in effort or intensity could prove fatal to their championship dream.

"We have made strides, especially on defense, but we can be even better on both ends of the floor," Roberts said. "We just need to continue to come out with a lot of intensity because every team is going to play us tough."

23 DRAGON SLAYERS

So much attention is given to the stars of a team, and rightfully so; but, as the Oilers prepared to go on the road to take on Tiffin University, a first-year team in the GLIAC located about twenty miles east of Findlay on State Route 224, I decided to write my game preview around Wilhite, who was battling back from a knee injury that had been bothering him since his high school days at Cincinnati Lockland. Wilhite had arthroscopic surgery on his knee in December and wore a brace because of it. He did what he could to fight through the pain and be a solid role player for the top-ranked team in the nation.

"It's a special year," Wilhite said, the week of the game. "I'm just trying to fit in and play my role so that I can help us get a championship ring."

The pursuit of a national title is what drove every player on this Findlay team and, because of it, Wilhite, didn't care that he was playing with an injury.

"It was pretty jacked up," Wilhite said, of the inside of his knee. "I had a partially torn meniscus and some torn cartilage. I'm trying to get back in shape and build my confidence up to make more moves on it."

The drawback to his injury was it chased off recruiters while he was in high school. Wilhite, a four-time All-Miami Valley Conference selection at Lockland, initially planned to play Division I college basketball.

"Corey Farley, who used to play here told me about Findlay and I was like 'Findlay?' I'm not about to go to a Division II school."

Anyone close to Division II basketball will tell you how good the quality of play is. Many D-II players are good enough to go Division I but are overlooked for a variety of reasons. They aren't tall enough, fast enough or strong enough or injuries prevent them from getting to the Division I level. Wilhite, who sadly passed away in 2013, was thankful he came to Findlay and Niekamp was as well.

"Antoine isn't completely healthy yet but he is giving a good effort and helping the team," Niekamp said. "He is learning what playing at this level is about."

Tiffin was still learning how to survive in the GLIAC. The Dragons had been roughed up in their first fifteen games, losing fourteen times, and they were winless in ten GLIAC games. They had lost twelve consecutive games coming into their battle with the Oilers and were led by junior guard Alex Strok, who was averaging 12.6 points per game. As a team, the Dragons were putting up 61.3 points per game and giving up 83.6. The Dragons, who had lost their last twenty-one games to the Oilers, were dealing with a baptism by the hottest fire imaginable in their first season in the conference.

"It's been an adjustment coming into this league," said Rodney Martin, who was the head coach at Tiffin at the time. "We played some of the GLIAC teams last year, but now it's a day-to-day thing. I've told the guys playing Findlay is like any other game. You have to go out and play hard. We look forward to the challenge."

For a team such as Tiffin, which was a long way from playing in the postseason, playing Findlay was the equivalent of playing in a national championship game. The Oilers, who had just tied the 2001-02 team for the best start in program history at 14-0 in their last win, could not afford to take the Dragons lightly.

"I can tell you this, Tiffin will be ready for the Oilers," Niekamp said. "They have capable players. We need to not only start strong, we need to avoid having a drop-off in how hard we play."

As I made the short drive over to the Gilmor Center, I thought about how this season was shaping up to be something special. The Oilers were past the midway point of the regular season and showed no signs of allowing the grind to get the best of them. Playing inside the Gilmor Center, which barely seats 1,000 fans and is smaller than most high school gyms I've covered games in, is not an easy thing to do. The crowd is right on top of you, and if things don't go right for the visiting team, the noise of the crowd forces teams to lose focus. The Oilers were challenged early, leading just 22-17 near the midway point of the opening half. A 14-2 run capped by two free throws from Bostic, gave Findlay the breathing room it needed as it surged in front 36-19. Parker was instrumental in the success of the Oilers in the early going, attacking the basket at will and creating opportunities for short jumpers in the lane. He also drilled a 3-pointer and made an effort to kick the ball out to open teammates. His performance helped the Oilers roll into halftime with a 51-29 advantage.

"We weren't going to take them lightly no matter what their record was," Parker said. "Every team is gunning for us because we have a target on our back. We have so many guys that can step up."

Parker torched the Dragons for 18 points, 17 coming in the first half, and he also tallied three assists and two steals.

"Marcus was very effective," Niekamp said.

Dealing with Parker is tough enough. He is quick and can beat you off the dribble with ease. His ability to either score or dish the ball off is what makes him such a headache to defend. Not to mention the fact that he is an aggressive defender, forcing opponents into mistakes on a consistent basis. Perhaps if the Dragons only had to worry about Parker, they would have been in good shape. The problem was they had to deal with other Oilers stepping up. The Dragons had to deal with Lewis scoring 16 points and handing out seven assists. They had to put up with Bostic pouring in 16 points and racking up five steals and they had to deal with Roberts and Sparks scoring 13 points apiece. Sparks turned in a double-double as he added ten rebounds and Roberts grabbed eight rebounds. The Oilers dominated the boards, holding a 46-27 advantage. The complete performance added up to a 106-65 win, marking the Oilers' first 100-point game of the season. The Oilers hit the century mark when Evans scored on a layup with less than two minutes remaining. He then nailed an NBA-range 3-pointer to finish off the Dragons.

Findlay's teamwork was phenomenal. The Oilers dished out 21 assists and lit the nets on fire, shooting a sizzling 61.5 percent from the field. Tiffin shot 40 percent from the floor and Darnell Patterson scored 21 points to pace the Dragons. The biggest problem for Tiffin was that it struggled to take care of the basketball. The Dragons turned the ball over twenty times as the Oilers reminded everyone why they were one of the nation's best defensive teams.

"We expected Tiffin to play hard," Parker said. "The key was keeping our composure and running our offense. We also played hard on defense. We know if we play hard on defense, good things are going to happen."

The Oilers improved to 15-0, their best start in the history of a program rich in tradition and success, and they still owned the real estate at the top of the national poll. They were 11-0 in the GLIAC. As I drove home from Tiffin, I thought maybe, just maybe, it was possible for the Oilers to get through the regular season without a loss. The next stop for Findlay was a road game against in-state rival Ashland University on Saturday at Kates Gymnasium. No love was going to be lost between the Oilers and Eagles.

24 REVENGE IN THE RIVALRY

Findlay and Ashland started playing basketball against each other during the 1910-11 season and, lately, the rivalry had become a rivalry in the geographical sense only. The Oilers had won twelve of the last thirteen meetings against the Eagles heading into their Jan. 24 showdown and they held a 50-25 lead in the all-time series; still, records mattered little when the Oilers and Eagles hooked up. Ashland was struggling, sporting a 7-9 record overall and a 5-9 mark in the conference. A year earlier, the Eagles handed the Oilers an 84-81 loss at Kates Gymnasium. It ended the Oilers' twelve-game win streak against the Eagles and the loss had a lot to do with the fact that Findlay couldn't buy a 3-point shot to save its life. Findlay missed twenty-seven shots from beyond the arc. Niekamp decided to use that loss as motivation, pulling out the game tape from it and making his team relive the nightmare.

"It was a sickening feeling, seeing how badly we shot the ball," said Evans, who was one of the few players who actually made a 3-point shot in that loss.

The Oilers were determined to avoid a repeat of history, although they found themselves in a jam early, trailing 26-16 ten minutes into the game. The Eagles were an up-tempo team, averaging nearly 80 points per game, and they found a way to back the Oilers into a corner. Momentum would soon shift in the other direction. Bostic drilled a jumper, sparking a 19-3 run that ended when he stole the ball from Ashland guard Brett Wackerly near mid-court and turned it into an easy layup and a 30-29 advantage. The Oilers took a 38-36 lead into halftime against an Eagles team that had pushed them as hard as any opponent had all season.

Six minutes into the second half, Ashland was still hanging around and only trailed 52-43. The Oilers had to make a move to take control. Enter Evans, who hit a trey that put the Oilers in front by 12. That shot was just what the Oilers needed to get on a roll. Six more 3-pointers followed, including a stretch where Hyde hit two and Evans and Parker each knocked down one as the Oilers stormed in front 74-53. Evans made three treys and the Oilers made a total of nine in the second half. They were 12-of-22 overall from long distance, a statistic that served as the difference maker in an 84-65 win. Findlay had avenged the painful loss from a year ago and left Ashland shaking their heads in disbelief.

"I thought the key was we got the ball to our high percentage shooters," Niekamp said, in a post-game interview. "And when you are making 3's, it not only energizes you on offense but it energizes your play defensively."

Indeed, the defensive play of the Oilers was on point. Wackerly, known as Ashland's sharp-shooter, did score 18 points but he managed to hit on only one of his six attempts from 3-point range. Kale Richardson, a sophomore post player and a rising star, led the way with 20 points.

"I thought we did a good job on Wackerly," Niekamp said. "He is an excellent shooter and we made him work for his shots."

It wasn't just that the Oilers were able to hit shots, their ability to play hard and play smart made a difference after struggling early to get on track.

"We started slow but Ashland is a good team," Bostic said. "The key was picking up our intensity and communicating better on defense. Everything came together after that."

Bostic scored 14 points and moved into a tie for twenty-first on the all-time scoring list with 1,304 points. Roberts finished with 15 points and did a tremendous job of taking away second-chance opportunities for the Eagles by grabbing eight rebounds. Hyde led the Oilers with 17 points and Parker scored 11 to go along with six assists. Lewis added 10 points as Findlay's balance on offense was too much for Ashland to handle. The Oilers could have easily stubbed their toes against the Eagles but they managed to survive another test and come away with another big road win. Findlay was 16-0 overall and 12-0 in the GLIAC. Its lead in the South Division was at six games with ten to play.

"It feels good to be closer to the title. Winning the South is the first thing we set out to do," Bostic said. "We have to take each game as it comes and let everything else fall into place."

What was impressive about Findlay at this point in the season was it refused to get caught up in the seductive excitement and hype of being the top-ranked team in the nation. Unbeaten records have a way of disappearing this late in the year, The Oilers avoided that pitfall. Staying on course would become a little more challenging as they moved forward. The Oilers were about to make their second lap through the conference schedule, and the stakes would be higher because the NCAA regional rankings were on the verge of being released. The top eight teams in the regional poll at the end of the season earned an NCAA tournament berth, with the top team hosting the regional. The Oilers knew the value of playing at home and wanted to make sure they were in a position to be there for the regional.

25 CLOSE CALL IN THE UP

Findlay was scheduled to play Central State on Jan. 27 but a snowstorm postponed that Tuesday night game until a later date. It would prove to be a blessing in disguise because the bonus off day would give the Oilers a little extra rest and a little extra time to prepare for a crucial two-game road stretch in Michigan, starting with a Thursday night game against Lake Superior State in Sault Ste. Marie. The long trip, coupled with the fact that the Oilers would be playing the Lakers on their home floor, would test Findlay mentally and physically. Playing on the road often forces teams to rely more on their ability to defend rather than their ability to shoot the ball well. Shots don't always fall on the road but defense can be a constant no matter where the game is played. Findlay leaned heavily on its defense and was one of the best when it came to coming up with steals. The Oilers averaged nearly eleven steals heading into their game against the Lakers, ranking 15th in the nation in the category.

"Stealing is the key to our defense," said Parker, in an interview after practice that week. "We pressure the ball and are relentless."

Parker was one of the best at forcing turnovers. He had racked up twenty-six steals and ranked sixth in steals per game in the conference, averaging 1.6 per game. Bostic and Lewis ranked first and second, respectively, in steals per game in the conference. Bostic averaged 2.6 and had come up with 41 while Lewis averaged 2.4 steals per outing. He had tallied 38. Bostic explained in an interview the reason why he and his teammates were so good at stealing the ball.

"I would say it's all about positioning," said Bostic, a two-time All-GLIAC defensive team selection. "We really work at being in the right spot in practice. It works and we stick with it."

With Bostic, Lewis and Parker leading the way, the Oilers had forced ten or more steals ten times in the first sixteen games and were ranked second nationally in turnover margin, plus 6.2. Of the 290 turnovers the Oilers had forced through sixteen games, 168 were off steals. Ernst, who as I've said before, played a crucial role in preparing the Oilers to be at their best defensively, offered this insight on Findlay's knack for stealing the ball.

"We teach discipline but error on the side of aggression," Ernst said. "We are one of the few teams in the conference that does some pressing and trapping to complement our man-to-man defense."

Ernst also shared his thoughts on the defensive success of Bostic, Lewis, and Parker.

"They are all quick, athletic and play with great motors," Ernst said. "They have the ability to cover mistakes with their effort and athleticism on defense."

Defense was going to be crucial against the Lakers, who were on a roll as they prepared for their battle with the Oilers. Lake Superior had won nine of its last ten and sat atop the North Division standings with a 9-3 record in the GLIAC. The Lakers were 12-5 overall and were a dangerous 3-point shooting team, shooting better than 40 percent from long range. Senior guard Mark Morse was the top shooter for the Lakers, having connected thirty-nine times from long range. He was one of three players on the team that had made at least 20 3-pointers. Senior guard Tim VanOudheusden led the Lakers in scoring, averaging 18.5 points per game, while senior forward/center Ryan Kuhl was coming into the game clicking for 13.2 points per outing. The Oilers had every reason to be concerned with playing the Lakers, who were a different team than the one that got hammered 73-55 at Croy Gymnasium in December.

"They are a veteran team that probably feels like they are at a good point in their season," Niekamp said. "They have an exceptional 3-point shooting team. They also have a strong inside game. It will present a challenge for us."

Not only did the Oilers have to worry about avoiding an upset, they were also playing with the added pressure of being the top team in the first NCAA Midwest Regional poll of the season. Bellarmine, out of Louisville, was second, two games behind the Oilers in the loss column. Southern Indiana, Northern Kentucky, St. Joseph's (Ind.), Grand Valley, Rockhurst and Kentucky Wesleyan rounded out the top eight. Findlay worked hard to earn the top spot and didn't want to do anything to lose its grip on it.

"We have made strides and need to continue to do that," Niekamp said. "The teams that continue to improve and build on their momentum are the teams that have the most success."

No team is perfect forever and, as the first half wore on inside Bud Cooper Gymnasium, it was beginning to look like the Oilers would lose. Lake Superior played with fire in its eyes, fueled by a surge of energy that knocked the Oilers off track early. The Lakers led 28-13 on the strength of solid outside shooting. The Oilers knew if they fell any further behind, a comeback would be next to impossible. Findlay fought back with under ten minutes to play in the opening half, closing on a 17-7 run. Bostic, with a defender draped all over him, drilled a 3-pointer as time expired and the Oilers trailed 35-30 at halftime. It could have been worse. The Oilers shot only 37 percent from the field and went three-of-twelve from beyond the arc. At least now, with the deficit down to five, hope was alive.

"We weren't finishing shots inside and we couldn't hit 3-pointers," Niekamp said. "I think it was important to get the deficit down before the half. We told the guys we needed to find a way to hang in there in the second half."

The Oilers did hang around. Ten minutes into the second half, they took their first lead as Laflin hit a free throw for a 45-44 advantage. The lead changed hands seven times before Bostic knocked down a 3-pointer to put the Oilers in front 67-64. The trey was one of two he made in the final five minutes. Findlay was solid on defense, too, allowing only two shots from the field in the last five minutes. Hyde took care of the rest, scoring seven points in the final minute, including five from the line, as the Oilers scratched and clawed their way to a 76-72 victory. Instead of stumbling, the Oilers were now 17-0 overall and 13-0 in the GLIAC. Bostic moved into a tie for 18th on the all-time scoring list with 1,328 points after scoring 24 points in this rugged battle of GLIAC division leaders.

"Josh made some big plays at the end and Nathan sealed the win with his free throws," Niekamp said. "I thought we showed a lot of poise at the end in a very tough situation."

The win was a testament to the mental toughness of the Oilers and their ability to persevere in the face of adversity. Had they stubbed their toe against the Lakers, it would have gone down as an upset, but realistically, a loss wouldn't have surprised anyone who understood the difficulty of winning on the road in college basketball. Lake Superior shot 56 percent from the field, hitting seven 3-pointers, and got 26 points out of VanOudheusden. Kuhl scored 22 points. Most teams would have succumbed against that type of effort by an opponent. Findlay wasn't most teams.

"Every game is a chance to learn something about your team," Niekamp said. "Tonight, we learned that, No. 1 Lake Superior is a very good team and, as No. 2, we gave a pretty good effort to come out of here with a win."

Findlay would have little time to enjoy the win. The players had to get back on the bus and head over to the team hotel for the night before heading to University Center in the morning for a game against

Saginaw Valley State. The Oilers were set to play the Cardinals on Saturday at the Ryder Center. Findlay was going to have to dig deep again to survive another grueling test on the road.

26 SURVIVAL IN SAGINAW

It had been less than forty-eight hours since Findlay ground out a win over Lake Superior and, now, the Oilers needed every bit of energy they had left to get past the upset-minded Cardinals. While the Cardinals were 5-12 overall and 5-8 in the league, a win over the Oilers would make their season. The Cardinals had won three of their last four games but, even on a day when the Oilers could feel the wear and tear of a long season taking its toll, they weren't going to let a lack of energy lead to their downfall.

Bostic made sure of it. He was unreal in the opening half, lighting up the scoreboard for 23 points and staking the Oilers to a 48-31 lead at halftime. Bostic highlighted his performance by knocking down a huge jumper and scoring on a free throw after being fouled on a layup that went in as well. A 3-pointer by Hyde also helped fuel a first-half surge that gave Findlay a 17-point lead at the half. Baskets were much tougher to come by in the second half as the Cardinals began to close the gap. Saginaw Valley trailed 51-41 with just under fifteen minutes to play before Sparks came through with two big-time plays. He scored on a layup first to push the lead back to 12 and then stole the ball and took off the other way for a dunk. The Oilers went up by 20 when Laflin drilled a 3-pointer. Then there was Bostic, once again looking every bit like the frontrunner for National Player of the Year honors as he finished with 31 points and moved into 17th all-time on the school scoring list with 1,359 points. Bostic added thirteen rebounds and four steals as the Oilers rolled to an 80-58 win.

"Sometimes you have big games like that," Bostic said, in a post-game interview inside Findlay's locker room. "My teammates set good screens and found me open for shots. I just rode with it."

What was impressive about the win, particularly since it was earned in relatively convincing fashion, was the Oilers were able to overcome a lack of energy, which came with the territory of having played six of their last ten games on the road. No one, however, was going to feel sorry for the Oilers, who were 18-0 overall and 14-0 in the GLIAC.

"Mentally, it's not that hard to get up for another game but, physically, you feel drained a bit," said Bostic, who, like his teammates, looked visibly worn down. "Every team is going to give us their best shot. You just have to suck it up. It's all part of playing hard and trying to win a championship."

Niekamp was particularly impressed with how Bostic handled himself, noting his senior star had the look of a player who knew his time was limited as the regular-season finish line came into sight.

"Josh played very well," Niekamp said. "He is

playing like a senior heading down the stretch run of the season."

Hyde added 12 points and Parker scored 10. With the win, the Oilers were now a heartbeat away from wrapping up the South Division championship. Findlay had a seven-game lead over Ashland and Hillsdale with eight games left.

"We just have to keep grinding and improving our game," Bostic said. "There are no easy games. We are going to have to fight hard to win every one of them."

The next two games were at home, starting with a showdown against Grand Valley on Thursday night. The Lakers had beaten the Oilers three times the previous season and, with only one win against the Lakers so far this season, Findlay still believed it wasn't done dishing out revenge.

27 REVENGE PART 2

It's easy to lose focus during the grind of a long season, especially for a team ranked No. 1 in the country. Players start buying into the hype a little more and sometimes let up from an intensity standpoint because they believe showing up on a game day is enough to produce a win. The Oilers didn't allow anything to blur their vision. One game at a time was more than a cliché. It was the Oilers' mission statement. Having three seniors in the starting lineup and two other seniors coming off the bench played a crucial role in the Oilers' ability to stay focused.

"We know if we take care of business, everything else will fall into place," Lewis said. "We take each game as it comes, putting all of our effort into that game before moving on to the next one."

Niekamp was impressed with how well his team had handled everything that came with being No. 1 in the nation. "They have been through this before and they understand the importance of taking it one game at a time," Niekamp said. "Up to this point, we have done a good job of keeping our focus."

The Oilers had to remain focused if they were going to beat Grand Valley in a game that was important to the conference race and region as well. The Lakers were 15-4 overall and 10-4 in the GLIAC. They were ranked fifth in the region, while the Oilers entered the game still holding the top spot.

"They have a great program with very talented players," Niekamp said. "We learned last year just how good they were as a team."

Grand Valley had lost just twice in its last eleven games, running off six consecutive wins during the stretch. Ringler was still the top threat, averaging 13.4 points and 6.6 rebounds per game, and the Lakers were the top shooting team in the conference, knocking down 50.8 percent of their shots.

"They have improved considerably since we last played them," Niekamp said. "They are probably the most physical team in the league and the best rebounding team in the league."

Findlay was riding the high of a successful road stretch where it won four consecutive games, no easy task in the rugged GLIAC. Five players were averaging 10 or more points per game, including Bostic, who was averaging 17.9. The Oilers were an offensive machine, cranking out 81.8 points per game. I was able to get up with Wesley for a phone interview the week of the game. I asked him to share his thoughts on the Oilers. Wesley had a pretty good perspective on perfect teams as his Lakers were perfect during the regular season a year earlier.

"We have tremendous respect for Findlay," Wesley said. "They have outstanding players and have a great chance to run the table in the league. They handled us rather easily earlier in the year. It's obvious why they are the No. 1 team in the country."

With a win over the Lakers, the Oilers would clinch the division title. A win would also move the Oilers one step closer to securing home-court advantage for the conference tournament in March. Games against Grand Valley had become a big deal, especially since 2007 when the Lakers rose to prominence by reaching the Elite Eight for the first time. The Student Oiler Club planned to make the atmosphere of the game match the importance of it by organizing a White-Out at Croy Gymnasium. As expected, nothing came easy for the Oilers even though they raced out to a 22-9 lead early in the first half; but the bruising, physical style of play the Lakers employed to attack teams lured the Oilers into foul trouble. Grand Valley was right back in the game because of it. The Oilers led 32-28 at halftime.

The Oilers tried to pull away in the second half. They led 38-28 out of the gate, but the Lakers didn't back down. Behind the stellar play of Trammell, who scored 19 points, the Lakers hung around and the raucous crowd of nearly 2,000 was on the edge of its seat as the final intense-filled minutes played out. With a minute to go, a mad scramble for the ball took place on the floor near the Grand Valley basket. Lewis and Parker were in on the play for the Oilers, who were clinging to a 59-57 lead. Parker was fouled amid the madness and hit two clutch free throws to put Findlay back in front by four points. Moments later, Bostic pulled up for a jumper from about fifteen feet and nailed it, whipping the 1,861 fans into a frenzy, as Findlay extended its lead to 63-57. The shot drove a dagger through the heart of the Lakers, who played so hard for so long in an extremely difficult environment but fell 69-62. Bostic joked after the game about seizing the moment in a pressure-packed situation.

"That shot better've went in," Bostic said, with a laugh. "The floor was spread out and it was my opportunity to take it. Croy is a special place and being able to make that shot in this situation is one of the reasons I signed on to play basketball here."

Bostic carved up the Lakers for 22 points and came up with eight rebounds and three steals as well. The Oilers were champions of the South Division for the seventh time in eight seasons. The game wasn't pretty, although more often than not, wins never are against Grand Valley. Findlay shot only 21.1 percent from 3-point range and was one-of-eleven from beyond the arc in the second half. It also turned the ball over fifteen times. In the end, the less-than-stellar statistics mattered little. Findlay was 19-0 overall and 15-0 in the conference.

"It was a great game and it came right down to the wire," Lewis said. "We made big plays at the end, getting some rebounds and hitting some free throws. We know there is a lot we can clean up but a win is nice no matter how ugly the game is."

Two others finished in double figures, with Lewis scoring 12 points and Roberts finishing the night with 11 points.

"We didn't shoot the ball well at all but we still won and that is a plus," Niekamp said. "It was probably good for us to be tested. There haven't been a lot of games where we've had to fight possession by possession the last couple of minutes."

As big of a win as it was, the Oilers had little time to enjoy it. Ferris State was up next.

28 BIG WIN OVER BULLDOGS

If there were any concerns about a letdown against the Bulldogs, they faded fast Saturday afternoon. Parker worked himself open for a 3-pointer to snap a 4-4 tie and the Oilers maintained control of the momentum most of the first half. Ferris State stuck around thanks to the play of Keenan, who helped his team close the gap to 30-27 with seven minutes remaining. Findlay managed to stay a step ahead and went into halftime with a 43-31 lead. When Parker knocked down a trey with fifteen minutes left in the game, the Oilers owned a 56-38 lead and were on their way to a victory. The end result was a convincing 85-62 win, thanks in large part to Parker, who rose to the occasion, scoring 17 points, hitting three treys along the way, and dishing out six assists.

"Marcus got some good looks against their zone defense and hit a couple of 3's that took them out of their zone," Niekamp said, in an interview. "We have so many different guys that can score. Tonight, it was Marcus' turn."

One of his signature moments in the game was a lob pass to a leaping Lewis in the second half. Parker brought the ball up the floor and threw it in the air for Lewis, who threw down a thunderous dunk over Keenan. For Parker, the play was business as usual.

"I've been doing that since I got here," Parker said, outside the locker room. "It's a crowd motivator. It gets everyone on their feet and gives us energy."

Parker had the daunting task of defending talented Ferris State point guard Darrien Gay and he did a remarkable job. He limited Gay to 5 points on 2-of-8 shooting from the field. Gay came into the game averaging 11 points per outing.

"Their point guard is lightning quick. You have to guard him tight," Parker said. "I was trying to pressure the ball and keep them from getting the ball inside to Keenan."

Keenan played well despite having trouble getting his hands on the ball. The 19-leading scorer in the country poured in 25 points, although he was forced to earn every point he got against the Oiler, who opted not to double team him.

"He is a tremendous player," Niekamp said of Keenan. "We didn't want to double-team him. We guarded everyone else as well as we could and I thought our depth wore on them."

Indeed, as had been the case so many times this season, the depth of the Oilers played a crucial role in the outcome. The Bulldogs couldn't match it. Donte Molden was the only other player in double figures for Ferris State as he scored 10 points. The Bulldogs shot 42.1 percent from the field and turned the ball over twenty times. Bostic continued his torrid pace, hanging 22 points on the Bulldogs. He had now scored 99 points in four games and also dished out five assists, including three in the final minute of the opening half. On one of those assists during the stretch, he acted as if he were going to take a shot before zipping the ball inside to Roberts, who slammed it home to help the Oilers keep their double-digit lead. Bostic tallied five steals as well while Hyde scored 13 points.

It wasn't a perfect win as the Oilers did turn the ball over fifteen times. In the end, that didn't matter as Findlay won its 20th game of the season, the eighteenth time that Findlay had won at least twenty games under the direction of Niekamp, who was pleased with how his team responded less than forty-eight hours after holding off Grand Valley.

"We had a lot of different guys shoot the ball well," Niekamp said. "I also thought we played with a lot of energy after a tough game against Grand Valley and I think that is a credit to our depth."

29 TOPPING THE TIMBERWOLVES

Sometimes it's easy to overlook the importance of role players but, at Findlay, they were one of the reasons the Oilers had gotten this deep into the season without a loss. Agunga was among them and talked about the strength of the Findlay bench during an interview the week of the Oilers' game against Northwood at Croy Gymnasium. I asked him about having to come off the bench and deal with some of the top players in the league, such as Keenan. In the most recent win against Ferris State, Agunga played ten minutes and helped defend the Bulldogs' intimidating center. Having to go up against Keenan didn't bother him because he defends great players in practice every day.

"I know if I can stop JB or Lee, I can handle defending anyone," Agunga said. "Playing against them gives me a lot of confidence."

His confidence rising throughout the season, Agunga had seen action in fourteen games, scoring 19 points and grabbing fifteen rebounds and he was on the right track after being bothered by a shoulder injury at the start of the year and missing six games in January because of a knee injury.

"I'm getting back into shape and feeling more comfortable," Agunga said. "There is a lot I can improve on. I know I can hit the boards harder and I'm taking a lot of pride in playing good defense."

Niekamp was pleased with Agunga's progress and talked about his value to the team.

"He brings a lot of energy and enthusiasm to the floor," Niekamp said. "He is learning his role and finding things he can do to help the team."

The next challenge for Agunga and the Oilers was a Thursday night game against the Timberwolves, who were coming to town at 11-10 overall and 7-9 in the conference. More importantly, Northwood was coming to Ohio fighting for its postseason life. The Timberwolves entered this game tied with Ashland for the eighth and final spot in the GLIAC tournament, and while they had lost seven of their last ten games, it wasn't an excuse for Findlay to overlook them.

"I told our players they will give us their best shot," Niekamp said. "They have a lot on the line, just as we have a lot on the line as we head down the home stretch."

Northwood wasn't a high-scoring team, averaging 67.5 points per game, but it was a respectable defensive team, allowing only 64.2 points. Junior guard Chris Johnson was the leading scorer at 11.6 points per outing. The Timberwolves were also the best rebounding team in the league, grabbing nearly 37 per game. The Oilers were the top-scoring team in the GLIAC, putting up just over 81 points per outing, and were ranked fourteenth in the country in points, allowing 61.3. With one more win, they would have seventeen conference wins for the second time in three seasons. Much was on the line for the Oilers heading into this final stretch, including home court advantage in the NCAA Midwest Regional.

"This one of those seasons where you'll look back on it someday and say 'Wow,'" Agunga said, as we wrapped up our interview. "Right now, we're all living in the moment and trying to keep things going."

Lewis came into this game looking to get going again and helping the Oilers ring up their twenty-first win. He had scored only 31 points in the last four games, a quiet stretch for a talented and explosive player. He would own the night against Northwood, literally soaring back into the spotlight. He threw down a couple of rim-rocking dunks to highlight a sizzling 21-point performance as the Oilers dominated the Timberwolves 91-52. Findlay led 44-20 at halftime, stomping the confidence out of Northwood early, and shot a blistering 56.1 percent from the field in the victory. Lewis, who also added five rebounds and four steals to his stat line, said no one really cares who rises up on a given night. Winning is what matters.

"On this team, because we are so talented, it's tough for everyone to get points," Lewis said. "We always make the extra pass and do what is best for the team. Tonight happened to be my number and I hit some shots."

Lewis punctuated his effort with a pair of dazzling dunks in the second half. On one, he soared into the lane and threw down a one-hand jam that gave the

Oilers a 51-23 lead. Moments later, Lewis and Bostic were running the floor on a fast break. Bostic lobbed the ball into the air and Lewis jammed it home. The crowd roared as excitement buzzed through the gym.

"When we get out on a fast break, we have freedom with the ball and we try to make the best of it," Lewis said. "It's a lot of fun and the fans love it."

This win over the Timberwolves was a glaring example of how special this Findlay team was shaping up to be. Bostic scored 15 points and Hyde finished with 10. Lewis talked about the Oilers' knack for overwhelming an opponent with their array of weapons.

"It seemed like everyone was scoring in the flow of the offense," Lewis said, with a touch of confidence in his voice. "You think with Josh being the player of the year, he needs to have a big game for us to win. But that is why we are the No. 1 team in the country. We have so many weapons. Any one of us can step up."

Lewis wasn't being cocky. He was being real. The Oilers were a legit No. 1 team and the latest win proved as much. Not only did they thrive offensively but they were unforgiving on defense against the Timberwolves, as well. Northwood shot just under 36 percent from the field and turned the ball over eighteen times. Johnson was the only player in double figures. He scored 12.

"Johnson got in foul trouble early and never got his game started," Niekamp said. "I credit our defense for the trouble they had getting other players involved."

The Oilers were now 21-0 overall and 17-0 in the GLIAC, rolling up their 69th consecutive win at home in the regular season.

"We got good looks at the basket, defended well and held them to 20 points in the first half," Niekamp said. "There are a lot of positives we can draw on from this win. I thought our defensive intensity was top-notch. It wore on them."

For the Oilers, who had a Valentine's Day date with Wayne State Saturday at Croy, the win was a reminder of the focused approach they took into every game. "We are so focused right now and we meant business tonight," Lewis said. "We are out to prove we are the best every night."

30 BREAKING THE HEARTS OF THE WARRIORS

Wayne State was having a miserable season, a rarity for a program with a reputation of being one of the top teams in the GLIAC each year. The Warriors were 8-13 overall and 6-11 in the conference as they prepared to play the Oilers. On paper, this looked like an easy win for the Oilers, especially at home. The Warriors, though, weren't going to make life easy on their rival, and the Oilers learned that quickly in a sluggish start to the game. Every shot they took was off the mark, be it a layup, a short-range jumper or a shot from beyond the arc. For nearly seven minutes, the Oilers were ice cold and trailed 9-4. If there was any team the Oilers didn't want to fall too much further behind against, it was Wayne State, which was desperate to have something go right during a difficult season. Finally, the Oilers broke out of their slump. Sparks got an open-look from 3-point range, slicing the Warriors' lead to 9-7 with 13:08 to play in the half. The Warriors began losing momentum.

Bostic tied the game at 15-15. His shot ignited a 13-2 run that ended when Roberts, racing down the floor, took an outlet pass from Bostic and threw down a dunk for a 26-17 advantage. Findlay fans cheered and the Oilers rode the momentum to a 32-22 lead at halftime.

"It was perfect timing on that play," Roberts said, with a smile. "We needed a spark. It's always fun to make plays like that."

Roberts would play a pivotal role in helping the Oilers dominate the second half. With Findlay holding a 40-33 lead with twelve minutes to play, Roberts prevented the Warriors from getting to the basket. The effort by Roberts, along with a 19-4 run punctuated on a jumper by Bostic for a 59-37 lead, helped the Oilers roll to a 72-49 win. Standing in the hallway outside the Findlay locker room before the game, I noticed an extra bounce in Roberts' step as he ran out of the locker room for pregame warm-ups, music booming through the gym as the crowd settled in for another day of basketball. Roberts didn't put up eye-popping statistics, scoring eight points, grabbing five rebounds and blocking three shots, yet his energy and his effort on defense was crucial in the Oilers' latest win. Much of his defensive work focused on keeping Lawal in check. Lawal grabbed ten rebounds but only scored eight points. The Warriors needed Lawal to play well to have a chance. Roberts made sure it didn't happen.

"I knew I had to play solid defense and help crash the boards for us to be successful," Roberts said, after the game. "They have superb, big men but we got stops and that helped us get our offense going."

The importance of Roberts wasn't lost on

Niekamp, who was now the coach of a team that was 22-0 overall and 18-0 in the conference. The eighteen conference wins was a program record. Two years earlier, Findlay went 17-0 in the conference enroute to its first unbeaten season in GLIAC play.

"Lee is really improving himself, especially defensively, Niekamp said in an interview after the game. "He did a good job against a team that wanted to throw the ball inside. Lee was very valuable."

The Oilers didn't shoot lights out against the Warriors, shooting only 42 percent from the floor. They came into the game shooting 50.8 percent from the field. Good defense made up for it as the Warriors connected on only 36.8 percent of their shots and turned the ball over eighteen times. Bostic, once again, turned in a solid performance as he continued to live up to his hype. He scored 20 points and moved into thirteenth all-time on the school scoring list with 1,438 points. Lewis finished with 14 points and pulled down ten rebounds, as he rang up his second double-double of the year. The play of Bostic, Lewis and Roberts made up for the fact that the guards had a tough time getting on track against the Warriors. Hyde and Parker combined for only seven points on 2-of-12 shooting from the field.

"They came at us with a small lineup and got after our guards," Niekamp said. "They harassed us and we struggled to get organized on the offensive end."

Struggle or no struggle, the Oilers leaped over another hurdle on the road to perfection.

Findlay's regular-season win streak at home had reached seventy games and its final road trip of the regular season was up next, a trek to the Upper Peninsula for games against Michigan Tech and

Northern Michigan. To be undefeated this late was amazing; yet the journey was far from over.

"We have to stay hungry," Roberts said. "It's been great having the season we've had but we have to stay focused and continue to get better as a team."

31 IMPRESSIVE ROAD WIN

One final trip to the UP awaited the Oilers as they headed into the third week of February. A long and challenging trip awaited the Oilers, who weren't about to drive themselves crazy thinking about it. They were focused on the next game, a showdown with Michigan Tech Feb. 19 at the Student Development Center Gymnasium in Houghton.

"We get a lot of recognition but coach Niekamp makes sure we stay focused in practice, out of practice and in the classroom," Lewis said. "We even take DVDs of games home. It helps us prepare to the point where we know what teams are going to do before they do it."

Bostic said in the past he never bothered to take a DVD home. With the Oilers in the midst of a special season, he opted to take DVDs home often.

"It definitely helps," Bostic said. "We get to see tendencies teams have and we have a chance to go back and look at mistakes we've made and correct them."

Not only were the Oilers' basketball-related study habits on point, their drive and focus also had not been diminished by the blinding glow of success.

"It would be easy to look at 20-0 or whatever we are and be happy with it," Bostic said. "But we haven't won anything yet. We've won games, and that's all rah, rah, rah, but we don't have any hardware in the glass case yet."

Michigan Tech was 12-11 and 9-9 in the conference. The Huskies, though, despite a rare average year, were always one of the most disciplined teams in the league. They play smart and they play hard, and having the advantage of being at home against Findlay was huge. Springborn was the scoring leader for Michigan Tech, averaging 13.6 points per game. Frederick Bowe, a senior forward, was averaging 11.7 points and 7.9 rebounds per game. Heading into the game against Michigan Tech, the Oilers had won eighteen consecutive road games in the regular season and were averaging 81.3 points per game while allowing only 60.3. Still Niekamp knew his team had the potential to be even better.

"The good teams keep getting better and take their game to another level," Niekamp said. "This is what we are striving to do as we head into the final weeks of the season. The finish line is in sight. We have two tough games ahead of us this week. We need to dig down and find the energy to get two more wins."

Creating energy on the road isn't easy. The Oilers were ready to do it.

"It's always a tough trip to make, and we know they will play us hard," said Lewis, who was averaging 11.8 points per outing. "We are going to go out and play hard, too. This is the most focused this team has been in my four years here. We are ready to take our game to another level."

It did seem that as the Oilers inched closer to the postseason, they pushed even harder to be at their best. Unlike any other team I had covered in my career, this one had the "it" factor. The players made it known through their actions and words that this was their time and nothing was going to hold them back.

"This is the fun part of the year. Everything counts," said Bostic, who led the Oilers in scoring at 18.2 points per outing. "Coach Niekamp told us we still have some big fish to fry. It's time to go fry 'em."

Houghton is about six hours beyond the Mackinaw Bridge. It is a town where signs on the doors of gas stations warn snowmobile riders to take off their helmets before entering. Massive ice sculptures dot the landscape in the winter and skiing and ice fishing are popular in a unique and beautiful part of the country. Fans of the Huskies are passionate. The Michigan Tech pep band is made up of a unique cast of characters and the energy they bring to the atmosphere in the gym is unbelievable. They are loud, they give opponents a hard time and they help make the SDC Gymnasium one of the toughest places to play in the conference. The Oilers, though, talked all week about stepping up their game and they turned that talk into action once the game was underway.

Nearly nine minutes into the game, Michigan Tech was still as cold from the field as the ice that covers Lake Superior in the winter. Mike Hojnacki finally scored on a layup with 11:30 to play, making the score

11-5 in favor of the Oilers. Findlay soon surged in front 23-8 lead, and behind a relentless defensive effort, it stormed into halftime with a 33-12 advantage.

"They employed some unusual tactics against us, trying to spread things out and slow things down," Niekamp said. "I thought our team handled things superb and this game shows just how good we can be, defensively."

Michigan Tech suffered through a horrible shooting night, shooting only 26 percent from the field, and turned the ball over sixteen times. The end couldn't come soon enough for Michigan Tech, which was beaten down in a 64-36 loss. For the Oilers to win as easily and convincingly as they did was beyond impressive. It was the lowest point total for a Findlay opponent since the Oilers held Heidelberg to 34 points in an 88-34 win during the 2003-04 season. Findlay improved to 23-0 overall and 19-0 in the conference. Lewis enjoyed a perfect shooting night, hitting all eight of his shots from the field and scoring 17, including 15 in the first half. Bostic led the Oilers with 20 points. Roberts, who didn't make the trip with the team on Wednesday because he was battling the flu, turned in a gutsy effort after arriving in town earlier in the day, scoring nine points, grabbing two rebounds and blocking three shots in twenty minutes of work.

"There are a lot of difficult circumstances when you travel long distances for games. I think our veterans stepped up and played with the kind of maturity you need to win on the road," Niekamp said, after the game.

Findlay shot 50 percent from the field and

connected five times from 3-point range. Evans hit two of those 3-pointers. No one from Michigan Tech scored in double figures. "We didn't score a lot of points but you don't need to score a lot when you play defense the way we did tonight," Niekamp said.

Playing Michigan Tech is typically the tougher of the two games on the Upper Peninsula trip, mainly because of how successful the Huskies have been over the years. Then again, a game against Northern Michigan Saturday at the Berry Events Center in Marquette wasn't going to be a walk in the park.

32 SWEEP SUCCESS IN THE UP

The Oilers arrived in Marquette ready for their final road game against a Northern Michigan team that had dropped nine of its last twelve. The Wildcats were 11-13 overall and 6-14 in the conference but the Oilers had to be careful. Wounded animals are dangerous, and if Findlay didn't show up ready to go, failure was a real possibility. The Wildcats opted to attack from the outside out of the gate, launching up 3-pointer after 3-pointer. The first five were off the mark and Findlay capitalized, building an 18-7 lead. Renelique helped the Wildcats fight back, drilling three treys in a five-minute stretch and pulling the Wildcats to within 30-21 with five minutes left in the half. Parker answered, knocking down a couple of 3-pointers and turning a steal into a layup as the Oilers went into halftime with a 39-27 advantage.

Findlay had trouble putting the game away, leading 59-51 with under ten minutes left. An 18-10 run turned the tide for good. Parker delivered the final dagger as he hit a 3-pointer to put the Oilers in front

75-61 with a little less than two minutes remaining. Parker was the star on this day, scoring a career-high 22 points. His effort helped lift the Oilers to an 81-68 win and a perfect run through twelve road games. The importance of the accomplishment was not lost on Niekamp as his team prepared for the trip back to Ohio.

"You have to go through this type of travel to understand just how hard it is to win games like this on the road. You have to be mentally tough to handle it all," Niekamp said. "I told the guys it's a great accomplishment going 12-0 on the road. We feel good about what we've done."

The Oilers, still the No. 1 team in the nation and owners of the No. 1 spot in the region, once again leaned on veteran leadership, tenacious defense, and a balanced effort on offense to get the job done in a crucial road game. Findlay, which shot 50 percent from the field, held the Wildcats to 43 percent shooting and forced eighteen turnovers. The Oilers also cashed in on an offensive attack that featured four players in double figures. Roberts, only three days removed from a bout with the flu, stepped up and scored 13 points to go along with twelve rebounds. His effort helped the Oilers earn a 33-23 edge on the boards, which resulted in twenty second-chance points. Hyde scored 15 points and Lewis finished with 11. Renelique did all he could to keep Northern Michigan in the game, scoring 21, while McElroy and Warner scored 15 points apiece. The Wildcats played hard. In the end, the Oilers were the better team.

"Northern played with a lot of energy and never quit," Niekamp said. "Marc made some truly tough shots and they shot well as a team from the 3-point line; but I thought we handled their runs and took a lot of things away from them."

Findlay was headed home on the verge of a remarkable achievement. Three games were on the schedule for the final week of the regular season, starting with a Tuesday night makeup game against Central State. Not since the 1908-09 team had a Findlay team completed a regular season without a loss. As I prepared for the upcoming week, I was certain the Oilers would win all three games. Findlay was 24-0 overall, 20-0 in the GLIAC and knocking on the door of history. With three more wins, it would bust through.

33 MAULING THE MARAUDERS

Findlay was supposed to play Central State in January and had that game been played when it was scheduled, there is a good chance the Oilers would have been 24-1 instead of unbeaten. I don't think the Oilers would have lost to the Marauders. I do think, however, there was a real possibility they would have fallen victim to an upset against Lake Superior less than forty-eight hours later. Findlay barely escaped against the Lakers that January night in Sault Ste. Marie, rallying from a 15-point deficit to nail down the win. Not having to play two days earlier provided Findlay with extra energy to survive the test against the Lakers.

Playing Central State at the start of a big week wasn't going to be easy. The Marauders take pride in playing hard and were 19-8 heading into their game against the Oilers.

It was evident early Central State was going to push Findlay hard. The Marauders trailed 20-14 after a 3-pointer by Daryl Brownlee. Just when everyone thought the gap was closing, the Oilers stretched it back out with a demoralizing 18-4 run. It started with a 3-pointer by Sparks. Then Parker hit a trey. Evans knocked down a long-distance shot as well and the Oilers rolled in front 29-14 and took a 38-18 lead into halftime.

"That stretch gave us separation," Niekamp said. "We have a lot of different guys that can hit those (3-point) shots and I think it opens up dribble penetration and gives us a chance to get to the line. The combination of all three works well for us."

Central State didn't quit, even if it did trail the Oilers by 20. The Marauders battled back, cranking up their defensive intensity, pressing and trapping frantically. Robert Harris (22 points) and Cole Prophet (13 points, six assists) paved the way during the rally. With three minutes remaining, the Oilers were up 72-59 and hoping they could hold off a furious comeback attempt.

"They elected to press us and turn the game into a rat race," Niekamp said. "They matched our athleticism, and that is something a lot of teams can't do."

Niekamp was right. Most of the time, Findlay overwhelmed opponents with its athleticism. Central State was an exception, but even the Marauders weren't able to match it all the way, thanks in part to Bostic and Lewis. Bostic torched Central State for 20 points and also grabbed eleven rebounds and dished out seven assists. Lewis nearly came through with a double-double, scoring 17 points and pulling down nine rebounds. Roberts made an impact as well. He scored 12 points on an array of layups and dunks. The

Oilers also got to the line twenty-eight times and hit twenty-three free throws as they sealed the deal on an 87-69 win.

"We basically force teams to choose to guard us on the outside or try to stop us inside," said Evans, who nailed a couple of 3-pointers and finished with seven points. "It makes it tough on teams to defend us."

Sparks added 12 points and Parker scored nine while handing out five assists. The Oilers shot 52.7 percent from the field. Bostic, always willing to offer a colorful quote or two in an interview, talked about the Oilers' ability to beat teams with a balanced attack.

"My dad always says the proof is in the pudding," Bostic said, with a laugh. "It's nice having different guys that can step up. It wears on teams."

The Oilers had used their depth to wear another team down. Only two opponents remained as the reality of a perfect regular season sank in a little more.

34 ROLLING OVER THE RIVAL EAGLES

As tough as it is to get through a college basketball season, especially playing each team in the conference twice, logic tells you a team is going to get bitten by defeat at least once. Yet, here the Oilers were, on the cusp of history, ready to take on the Eagles for the second time this season. The loss to the Eagles a year earlier still burned in the minds of the players, in part because it was the only time in the career of the seniors that they had lost to Ashland. The night of February 26th couldn't get here soon enough for Findlay.

"We still feel like we owe them," Bostic said. "We know they are going to come in here hungry and we will, too. We like the flavor of Eagles, so we're goin' to have our dinner plates out and be ready to roll."

While the Oilers were poised to take another step toward perfection and preparation for the postseason, the Eagles were trying to keep their heads above water. Ashland was 10-14 overall and 8-12 in the conference. It had only a sliver of hope of earning a conference tournament berth as it sat tied for eighth with Wayne State in the standings.

"Ashland's going to come in here with their guns blazing and will be in do or die mode," Bostic said. "They have tremendous 3-point shooters. We have to be on top of our game."

Richardson had become a star for the Eagles and was playing his best basketball, averaging 18.6 points per outing. Wackerly was still a viable threat as well, putting up 14.5 points per game. The Eagles had made 112 3-pointers and were shooting 40 percent from beyond the arc. Findlay was gunning for its seventy-second consecutive win in the regular season on its home floor and cranking out 80.8 points per outing while allowing only 60.6. Of the twenty-five games Findlay had played, only four opponents managed to score 70 or more points. The Oilers were determined to run the table in the conference, just as they had done two seasons ago during a one-loss regular season. Findlay was also still vying for home-court advantage in the NCAA tournament and the only way to keep that dream intact was to continue winning. As if that wasn't incentive enough, there was also the rivalry factor.

"There is going to be a lot of intensity and a lot of energy on both sides," Evans said. "There's definitely extra motivation because every year I've been here, you could see it in the seniors' eyes—they want to beat Ashland."

You could feel the excitement building up inside Croy Gymnasium as a spirited crowd of 1,892 packed into the gym to watch the Oilers battle the Eagles. They found out early on that they weren't going to be disappointed by the performance of the home team. Findlay was fired up, maybe more than it had been all season and there was a reason for it. It all goes back to their preparation for the Eagles during the week.

"We all still remember that 84-81 loss at their place last year. We watched clips from that game this week and coach Niekamp let the last one run," Lewis said. "We watched the fans rush the court. It was extra motivation."

No doubt about it. The Oilers dominated early and stormed into halftime with a 45-31 lead. They thrived on big plays to build the cushion. Bostic jammed home a dunk with one hand. Hyde torched the net for three 3-pointers and Sparks was aggressive, driving into the lane for an off-balanced reverse layup. Hyde's 3-pointer right before the buzzer, a shot that sparked a loud roar from the crowd, put the Oilers in front by 14 at halftime. The second half was a formality. Findlay opened the half on a 21-8 run and pushed its lead to 36 at one point as they beat the Eagles 88-54.

"We knew a 14-point lead wasn't that big against a team like Ashland," Lewis said, as music boomed inside the Findlay locker room after the Oilers' 26th win of the season. "We buckled down, tightened up our shoes and played hard. We wanted to send a message."

Ashland was hoping to give Findlay's record a black eye but never had a chance to make it happen. The Oilers shot a blistering 55 percent from the field and held the Eagles to 37.1 percent shooting. Richardson, so important to the success of the Eagles, managed only eight points. Wackerly struggled, too, scoring seven points.

"That is a credit to our players for playing well on the defensive end," Niekamp said, in a post-game interview in his office. "We made them work for everything."

Forced to work hard offensively made it much more difficult for the Eagles to be effective on defense. Bostic carved up the Eagles for 18 points and also tallied five rebounds, five assists and three steals. Lewis burned Ashland for 19 points and pulled down ten rebounds. Roberts came through with a double-double as well, scoring 11 points and grabbing eleven rebounds. Inside the locker room, the players were on an emotional high, taking a few moments to soak in the thrill of beating their in-state rival for the second time this season. They also took a few moments to reflect on the position they were in, sitting forty minutes of basketball away from getting through the regular season without a loss. Findlay had blown its share of teams out, had won every road game and even won a few close games along the way. The Oilers had earned their right to celebrate. At the same time, there was still a lot of work to do and a lot more to accomplish.

"We've been talking about how things could be for our senior year for a long time," Lewis said, as he pointed to the potential this team had going into the season. "We have put a lot of work into this season and it's special to be a part of it. We haven't had a perfect season by any means, but good teams get wins no matter what."

The position the Oilers were in even left Niekamp in awe, which isn't easy to do because Niekamp had been coaching college basketball for more than twenty years, all winning seasons, and had won 540 games. He went into the season knowing the Oilers had the potential to be special. He just never imagined it would be this special.

"If you look at everything prior to the season, it looks absurd that we could go undefeated," Niekamp said. "A lot of things fell into place. More than anything, we've been consistent. We have been pretty good, not great, but pretty good each night. That is rare."

Rare was a good way to put it. Every team has that one-off night, but even on nights when the Oilers weren't at their best offensively, they could always count on their defense. Findlay had the perfect blend of players, from the leadership of the veterans and scoring threats who could rise to the occasion on any given night to the role players off the bench who could be counted on to step up when called upon. Tiffin was now the only team that stood between the Oilers and 27-0. Saturday's game against the Dragons was the regular season finale and senior day for Bostic, Lewis, Roberts, Evans and Laflin. As a writer, I knew the Oilers couldn't afford to look past Tiffin, even if, on paper, the Dragons looked like nothing more than a senior day sacrifice.

35 SENIOR DAY

On the afternoon of Feb. 28th inside Croy Gymnasium, I was confident I was going to see the Oilers complete a 27-0 run through the regular season. The energy and emotion built up among the crowd of 1,892 was thick enough to cut with a knife. Tiffin was a miserable 2-25 overall and only 1-21 in the conference. On paper, the game was a mismatch of epic proportions. On the court, the statement held true.

Hyde got the Oilers going, launching up and connecting on four 3-pointers, pushing the Oilers in front 26-4 in the opening nine minutes of the game. All that was left to be decided was the final score as the crowd roared to its feet. The Dragons struggled badly and trailed the Oilers 43-22 at halftime.

"In the first seven or eight minutes of the game, we guarded them very well and Nate hit some big 3-pointers," Niekamp said. "We built a big lead and we were able to maintain it."

The Oilers turned the final twenty minutes into a glorified scrimmage. Lewis had perhaps the biggest highlight of the game when he stole the ball and took off for the basket. He elevated in the lane and threw down a dazzling dunk that energized the crowd and put Findlay in front 56-26 mid-way through the second half. The Oilers put the exclamation point on a perfect regular season with a 77-50 win.

"It was a great atmosphere," Evans said, in a post-game interview as music and cheers echoed from inside the Findlay locker room. "Our fans are great and we didn't need any extra incentive to play hard because it was senior day. Nobody wants to play bad on that day."

Tiffin shot only 38.9 percent from the field and had a twelve-minute stretch in the first half where they made only two field goals. It took Tiffin nearly seven minutes in the second half to hit a shot. Findlay was in cruise control, shooting 51 percent and connecting eleven times from beyond the arc.

"We'll enjoy today and then come to practice tomorrow and get back to work," Laflin said. "Being undefeated is something we can all be proud of and it's fun to be a part of this team."

Having fun played a huge role in the Oilers' ability to get through twenty-seven games without a loss. The players enjoyed being the team with the biggest target on its back and took pride in being unselfish.

"It's hard to put into perspective," Niekamp said, as he sat in his office after the game late Saturday afternoon. "It wasn't something we talked about much and it wasn't anything we expected. The fortunate thing is we've been healthy. Our thoughts are on looking ahead and not looking back."

Evans, though, took a moment to talk about what the 27-0 regular season meant to him.

"We'll always say we were part of a team that went undefeated in the regular season, but we have to downplay it right now," Evans said. "We're already talking about the tournament. It's a fun time of the year. We have to get ready to get after it."

The journey had been nothing short of remarkable up to this point and I was at a loss to put it into perspective. For now, it was all about living in the moment, and the next moment for the Oilers was the opening round of the GLIAC tournament Wednesday night. Findlay was the top seed, and if it won its opener against Northwood, it would host the remainder of the tourney over the weekend.

36 TIGHT BOND

You can look at the stats of a team over and over again but it's what is beyond the numbers - the intangibles - that put teams in a position to contend for championships. Bostic, Lewis, Roberts, Evans and Laflin were the undeniable leaders of this Findlay team, each bringing something important to the table, and the bond they had forged over the course of the last four seasons had become unbreakable. The drive to succeed that burned inside of them was unstoppable. It's why the Oilers were still perfect despite carrying the weight of being the No. 1 team in the country. In an interview the week of the conference tourney opener, Bostic, remarkably humble despite being the preseason National Player of the Year, talked to me about the bond.

"The senior class and the rest of the guys, too, all have a tight bond," said Bostic, who was entering the postseason averaging 17.6 points. 6.4 rebounds and 3.1 assists per game. "We do a lot of things together socially, such as playing cards, and it shows on the court. We know each other's tendencies and moves. It plays a big part in our success."

Evans compared the bond to a marriage.

"Sometimes we get mad at each other and get on each other at practice but there are good times, too," Evans said. "Right now, we are all excited for each other and happy with what we've done so far."

One of the best things about being a sports writer is having a chance to watch athletes grow up over the course of their careers. One minute they are wide-eyed freshmen trying to figure out their roles; the next, they are leaders.

"The guys have grown up in a lot of ways and have matured," Niekamp said. "They have grown close but also have learned what to expect from each other. That is so important."

The seniors had won 109 games and lost only twelve times. They owned a 68-5 record against conference opponents, were part of two unbeaten runs through the GLIAC and had lost only once in sixty-four games at home. They had done a phenomenal job of carrying on the program's tradition of success, taking it to another level and, now, were set to take the next step in their quest to win a national championship.

"The will to win has so much to do with our success," Lewis said, as we talked after practice. "We're motivated. We don't take losing as an option."

To get an understanding of how strong the bond of the players was on this team, one only needed to look at Lewis and the heartbreak he dealt with during his career. Inside Lewis' locker there was a picture of his dad holding him long before he could ever dunk a basketball and it was Lewis' way of keeping his dad close to his heart, during this historic season.

"It's tough. I wish he could be in the stands like he used to be," Lewis said, allowing me to get a closer glimpse of his personal life. "But I get a little prayer in during the Star-Spangled Banner and I know he is here with me. He has been watching over our team."

On the days when Lewis seemed to miss his dad the most, his teammates were there to support him.

"We've all been through a lot, on and off the court, but my teammates have always been there for me. We have developed a brotherhood."

Laflin said his teammates' support was huge when he was fighting through his injury earlier in the season.

"Injuries are tough but they are part of the game," Laflin said. "You just have to get through it and having my teammates and coaches there for me when I was sitting out helped me do that."

As my interview with the seniors rolled on, we talked about their experience in the 2008 conference tournament. I could hear the hurt in their voices as they reflected on the loss to the Lakers. I could also detect the determination in their voices as they talked about making sure the trophy came back to Findlay for the first time since 2007.

"Looking ahead to the conference tournament, we know we have a lot of work to do," Roberts said. "I think we're focused. We feel like no one can get in our way of winning the title, except ourselves."

Staying focused meant forgetting about the previous twenty-seven wins.

"In some ways, the season is just beginning," Niekamp said. "I told the team everyone is 0-0 again."

I don't think anyone was concerned about the

Oilers' focus. They knew the stakes were raised and, while the ultimate goal was to win a national title, the Oilers first had to worry about taking care of business in the GLIAC tournament. Not winning the conference tourney would put Findlay in danger of losing the right to host the NCAA Midwest Regional.

"The team that went to the 2005 Elite Eight is the one everyone talks about," Bostic said. "We want to build off that and do our own thing. We have to take it one game at a time and not get ahead of ourselves. We can't look past anyone because anyone can be beaten in basketball."

Northwood was up first and the Oilers had every intention of taking the Timberwolves seriously.

37 GLIAC TOURNAMENT OPENER: NORTHWOOD

Findlay found itself in a dogfight six minutes into its game against Northwood, the score tied at 10-10. Back-to-back 3-pointers by Hyde and a 3-pointer by Parker pushed the Oilers in front 19-10 and it seemed as if momentum was on the side of the Oilers.

Turns out it wasn't. Findlay led 19-18 with a little more than seven minutes left in the half. Holding off the Timberwolves was only the beginning of the adversity the Oilers would face as a cruel twist of fate unfolded inside Croy Gymnasium. Sparks drove into the lane looking to score on a layup. He jump-stopped in the lane and fell to the floor and clutched his knee. The gym was silent as 1,749 fans looked on while the training staff attended to Sparks, who later learned his anterior cruciate ligament was torn and that he would be out for the remainder of the season.

The Oilers had been blessed with great health throughout a demanding season, save for a few minor injuries here and there; Sparks' injury could not have come at a worse time. Sparks was one the most competitive and hardest-working players on the team. The fear was his absence would deliver a blow to the Oilers' championship hopes.

When the game resumed, the Oilers did their best to stay focused. Bostic threw down a jam off a missed shot to put the Oilers up 25-22 and a layup by Roberts right before halftime gave Findlay a 33-26 lead. As far as first halves go, the one against the Timberwolves was average. Bostic helped Findlay take its game to another level in the second half, drilling a 3-pointer that put the Oilers on top 38-29 two minutes into the action. Two free throws by Lewis and a layup by Parker pushed the Findlay advantage to 42-29 and the route was on. Bostic fueled it, scoring 10 points in a seven-minute stretch, including a layup with ten minutes left that gave the Oilers a 58-40 cushion. Bostic hit two more 3-pointers down the stretch and Lewis energized the crowd with a dunk. The final points came from Schomaeker, who checked into the game for the first time with just minutes remaining. The fan favorite delighted the crowd by hitting a trey to seal the deal on the Oilers' 81-49 victory.

Bostic lit up the Timberwolves for 26 points, a sign he was ready to raise his game up a few notches for the postseason. Parker carved up Northwood for 18 points while Lewis scored 16 points and grabbed eleven rebounds. Hyde added 12 points. The Oilers made ten 3-pointers and shot 57.1 percent from the field as they tied a school-record with their 28th consecutive victory. Northwood had no answer for the Oilers in the second half and failed to make a basket in the final eight minutes.

"It's hard to stop this Oiler team," Bostic said, with undeniable confidence. "So many guys on this team can score and, when we click on defense, too, we are even tougher."

Niekamp talked about the sluggish first half and the change of direction the team made in the second half. "Mentally, we were out of it," Niekamp said, of his team's first-half performance. "I thought in the second half, we turned it up, executed better and played with more energy."

Lewis admitted the Oilers were a little lackadaisical, something stemming from Findlay having rolled over its last eight opponents in the regular season, winning each game by 20-plus points.

"We had some games lately where we've rolled over opponents and I think we had our heads up our butts a little bit," Lewis said. "Coach reminded us of that at halftime. We laid it all out there in the second half."

38 GLIAC TOURNAMENT SEMIFINAL: MICHIGAN TECH

With a couple of days until a GLIAC tournament semifinal against Michigan Tech, I decided to take a little time to talk with Bostic and Lewis, two players who would have to continue to play at their best if the Oilers were going to march forward in their quest for a title. There was little concern about either one not being at their best. Twelve times during the season, Bostic and Lewis each scored at least 14 points in a game and both players had double-doubles in the December win over Hillsdale.

"Bostic and Lewis look for each other on the court and that comes with playing together for four years," Niekamp said, in an interview two days before Findlay played Michigan Tech. "They can hurt teams in so many ways, and both players are unselfish."

Lewis, who was averaging 12.5 points and 5.9 rebounds per game, talked to me about the connection he and Bostic shared and he noted the connection was solid, in part because of their unmatched drive to win a national championship.

"If there is anyone I'm on the same page with, it's Josh," Lewis said. "We are both after a common goal and we know the easiest way to get it is with each other."

Bostic, the team leader in scoring at 17.6 points per game, echoed those thoughts.

"Our whole team has great chemistry but with Morgan and I, we know each other so well from playing together in the summer and being on the same team for so long," Bostic said. "It's fun being on a team with someone as good as you."

On any other team in the conference, Lewis would be the go-to guy. No two players complemented each other better than Bostic and Lewis. The competitive fire that burned in each one is what made them such a tremendous tag team. In an effort to add a little fun into the interview, I asked Bostic who would win between the two in a game of HORSE.

"I don't know," Bostic said, smiling and laughing as he started to answer the question. "I would say dunking-wise, he may have me but I got a few tricks up my sleeve, too."

To see those two go at it in HORSE, or even a game of 21, would be a treat because of their fierce competitiveness.

"We are always going at it, bumping, pushing, fouling, and talking junk," Lewis said. "You wouldn't even think we knew each other if you saw us in practice. That competitiveness definitely carries over to the games."

Dealing with Michigan Tech was next on the agenda for the Oilers. On the road since Feb. 25, the

Huskies were road-weary. They weren't expected to be in the final four of the tournament but made it after knocking off Hillsdale 69-64 in the opening round. They were at a disadvantage against the Oilers, especially having to play Findlay at Croy, but the Oilers respected the Huskies too much to take them lightly.

"We need to get back to fighting mode," Niekamp said. "That is one thing we talked about after the game against Northwood. We have to come out hungry and ready to play."

Bostic was as hungry as anyone as the Oilers took the floor for their showdown against the Huskies in front of a sold-out crowd on a Friday night, and he set the tone early, turning a steal into a dunk and drilling a jumper to help push Findlay in front 6-0. Michigan Tech, despite playing on tired legs, had too much pride to let the game get away from it that easily and tied the game at 9-9.

Then Bostic took over. One 3-pointer ripped through the net. And then another. One more trey fell through for good measure off the hands of Bostic as Findlay led 18-9 with ten minutes to go until halftime. Bostic's drive to the basket soon put Findlay in front 20-11. Michigan Tech wouldn't go away, though, and only trailed 31-25 at the half. The Oilers weren't out of danger yet but they soon turned the tide behind a stellar defensive effort to start the second half. For the first five minutes the Huskies failed to make a basket. The Oilers capitalized. Hyde nailed a 3-pointer, Lewis scored on a putback, Parker slashed through the lane for a layup and Roberts split a pair of free throws. The Oilers led 39-25 and the

Huskies knew they were in trouble. Luke knew it as well as anyone. He had seen this sort of thing happen before in games in this gym, and he was going to have to watch it happen again to his team. With less than ten minutes left, the Oilers were up 48-29 on the strength of a 17-4 run. Roberts capped the run with a jumper. Findlay never looked back and rolled to a 64-46 win to punch a ticket to the championship game for the third consecutive season. Bostic, the newly minted GLIAC Player of the Year, led the way, scoring 21 of his 27 points in the first half and making all four of his attempts from beyond the arc.

"That's why Josh is the player of the year in our conference," Luke said, as he stood outside of his team's locker room in the basement of Croy Gymnasium. "He's an unbelievable player."

Bostic, determined as ever, gave credit his teammates for his special performance. "Guys were setting screens for me and I was hitting shots," Bostic said. "It feels good when the shots are falling. It's also a blessing to be on a team where other guys can step up and get the job done."

Bostic wasn't the only one putting on a head-turning performance in the opening half. Springborn was every bit as good as Bostic. He hit five 3-pointers and scored 17 points in the first twenty minutes to keep the Huskies within striking distance.

"Everyone just kind of sat back and watched Robby and Josh put on a show," Niekamp said. "He is a tremendous player and Michigan Tech has a lot of pride in their program. We knew they weren't going to come in here and just roll over."

In the end, the depth of the Oilers overwhelmed the Huskies. While Springborn played out of his mind, Bostic's unreal effort was merely a bonus on a team with so many weapons. Roberts and Hyde scored 10 points apiece. Findlay was tough defensively as well as it held the Huskies to 33.3 percent shooting from the field. "They have too much depth and we couldn't maintain our level of intensity against them," Luke said. "You basically have to pick your poison against them. We knew it was going to take an exceptional effort to have a chance."

With the Huskies history, the Oilers, now 29-0, shifted their attention to their biggest rival as they prepared to take aim at their fourth conference tournament title in program history. Grand Valley State was up next after it defeated Lake Superior State 81-69 in the other semifinal. It was fitting the Oilers and Lakers would meet for the championship. After all, it was Grand Valley that dashed Findlay's dream of a title a year earlier. This game provided a shot at redemption and Bostic was as eager as a child on Christmas Eve as he talked about the upcoming battle.

"It's ring week," Bostic said. "We know it's going to be a battle. We are going to bring our swords, shields, and all of that stuff. It's going to be fun."

39 CHAMPIONS AGAIN

Lines formed outside both entrances of Croy Gymnasium nearly two hours before tip-off on a mild Saturday afternoon in early March. The crowds had been growing all year as the Oilers' win total rose, the fans sensing this Findlay team was on the cusp of something special, and no one wanted to miss an opportunity to witness one of the biggest moments of the year as the announced crowd of 1,999 packed into the gymnasium for the Oilers' championship battle with the Lakers, who were playing for the league title for the fourth consecutive season. The Oilers were making their third consecutive trip to the title game. Findlay and Grand Valley knew each other as well as any two teams in the league and nothing short of an intense, hard-fought game between the bitter rivals was expected. Even though Findlay had won both meetings in the regular season, the loss in the conference championship game in 2008 was still on the Oilers' minds. Their thirst for revenge needed to be quenched. A victory would not only give the Oilers a league title, it would also secure home court advantage in the NCAA Midwest Regional. Findlay was ranked first in the regional poll but the NCAA folks are hard to read sometimes, and the only way Findlay could guarantee the right to host the regional over Bellarmine was to win.

Parker helped the Oilers take a 6-2 lead on back-to-back layups before the remainder of the half turned into a struggle. Fortunately, Grand Valley wasn't much better offensively, although the Lakers led 22-17 after Alvin Storrs knocked down a 3-pointer with a little under five minutes to play in the first half. Findlay responded. Evans made a nice assist to Roberts, who threw down a dunk and lit up the crowd with energy as the Oilers cut the deficit to 22-19. The Oilers, unable to build off the momentum in the final minutes, trailed 27-24 at halftime. Findlay missed all seven of its shots from 3-point range in the first half and shot only 29 percent from the field overall.

"Grand Valley has a lot of athletic players, and they played great defense," Niekamp said. "We missed easy shots and that made the other shots tougher to make. We got into a rut and couldn't make anything. As poorly as we played, we were only down three at halftime."

That was indeed the bright spot as the deficit could have been much bigger. Four minutes into the second half, the Oilers were down 32-29. Roberts and Lewis answered for the Oilers, each scoring on layups as Findlay went in front 33-32. It was the first lead since early in the first half. The baskets by Roberts and Lewis proved to be the beginnings of a game-changing 24-5 run. Ahead 35-34, Lewis jammed home the ball off a missed shot and Laflin and Bostic connected from 3-point range as the Oilers surged in front 43-34. Evans drilled a 3-pointer as he got knocked to the floor with eleven minutes to go. Laflin buried a jumper and Parker hit a shot from beyond the arc. By the time Lewis made two free throws with just over eight minutes left in the game, the Oilers were sitting pretty with a 53-37 lead. The capacity crowd roared as the Lakers burned a timeout in the hopes of cooling off the Oilers, who had momentum on their side and a victory within reach. The timeout didn't help and the Oilers rolled to the finish line, dropping the Lakers 67-56 to capture the championship. As the fans cheered, the players celebrated, sharing high fives, exchanging hugs, and hoisting the trophy. For the first time during this remarkable season, it seemed as if the Oilers were slowing down for a moment to savor the success.

"It feels like we're on top of the world," Roberts said. "We're 30-0 and GLIAC champs but, you know, we aren't done yet."

Bostic talked about the road ahead in a post-game interview. He had been named the MVP of the tourney and moved into 10th on the all-time scoring list at Findlay with 1,573 points. The latest accomplishments further cemented his place as the greatest Findlay player of all time. Bostic was more thrilled, however, that Findlay had won the title after failing to win any trophy a year earlier.

"For us seniors, it's even more special," said Bostic, who scored just nine points but finished with 66 in three tournament games, 11 shy of the GLIAC tourney record. "It feels great to beat Grand Valley and to do it as an unbeaten team."

While Bostic was the MVP, Lewis was the star on this night. He scored 15 points and grabbed ten rebounds, earning a spot on the all-tournament team. Parker scored 15 points and was also named to the all-tourney team. The Oilers had one of their worst shooting performances of the season, shooting just under 39 percent but made up for it with great defense as they forced twenty turnovers. What was overlooked in the win was the impact Laflin and Evans had on the outcome. They combined for only 11 points but made shots at the right time. Great teams have benches that help keep things rolling at a steady pace and raise the energy level when the team needs a boost. Laflin and Evans did both.

"As a bench player, you want to come in and give your team a lift," Laflin said. "I was trying to make something happen. We had trouble shooting in the first half but we have a lot of good shooters. Eventually we knew we would start making shots."

Wesley could only shake his head in disbelief after watching his Lakers get dismantled in the second half. Torreau Brown scored 12 points to lead the Lakers.

"We felt like we could compete with these guys and I thought, in the first half, we did that," said Wesley, who would now have to wait and see if his team would make the NCAA tournament. "Our offense went cold in the second half. Their defense was good."

With the GLIAC tournament title secured, the Oilers were a lock to host an NCAA Regional as the No. 1 seed out of the Midwest Region. It would mark the third time in program history the Oilers would host the eight-team tournament.

40 GIVING BACK

As hectic and pressure-packed as the season was for the Oilers, they still found time to step away from basketball and make a difference in the lives of fourth and fifth grade students. Players from the team spent time each week in a couple of city schools that had a good number of children who didn't come from the best home situations and struggled in school. Sometimes the Oilers would play basketball with the students. Other times, they would read to them or talk to them about how school was going, while reminding them of the importance of staying on track in school. While it was the students who benefitted the most from having the players around, the Oilers also gained a great deal from the experience. "By going over to the school, we help motivate those kids and help them get through their week," Roberts said. "They get real excited when we come over there and it's fun making a difference in a child's life. Sometimes we'll read a book or just play basketball with them. They enjoy it."

The idea for the Oilers to become role models in schools started during the 2007-08 season, when Bostic began working with a fourth grader who moved to Findlay from Detroit. The star of the Oilers sat down with the child and his mother. He praised the mother for being the best single mom she could be, not only by doing what she could to raise her son right, but, also, by going back to school in an effort to have a better life. For Bostic to go above and beyond what was expected of him served as a shining example of his character.

"Josh has done a tremendous job," Ernst said. "Everything people say about him is good and they don't even bring up basketball. He has definitely made a difference in the lives of the kids he's worked with, as have our other players."

The program took off during the 2008-09 season as Ernst got in touch with Findlay City School guidance counselors Nancy Baxter and Lisa McClain about having players come in to work with students at Bigelow Hill and Washington Elementary Schools.

"Charlie has always thought doing community service with the basketball players and various schools would be a win-win situation for both," Baxter said, in an interview in 2009. "It has worked out well and it is amazing how Charlie has helped us out with everything he has on his plate."

Despite the extra time involved in making this program a success, Ernst pointed out it was worth it in every way. "A lot of these kids don't have a Dad or are in a bad situation in life but they deserve that chance to have someone there for them to be a positive influence," Ernst said. "They get through to the kids where maybe the school can't and give them something to look forward to every week."

Bostic, in the midst of leading the Oilers on their quest for a championship, said helping children was nothing new to him.

"My dad is a minister and I have done work with kids in the past at his church," Bostic said. "We treat those guys like little brothers or cousins and try to make them feel special. It gives you a lot of satisfaction doing something positive for the community."

One of the biggest impacts Bostic made on a student was when he helped him get into the routine of attending school every day. He had not been showing up all of the time and Bostic helped change that habit. He told the student to start coming each day and to make sure he gave a copy of his school schedule to Baxter. The student promised he would do it. The next day, Baxter had the schedule and the student got back on track with his attendance. Bostic, despite being in the Upper Peninsula of Michigan for a game, called after the shoot-around to make sure the student had kept his promise.

Lewis also took pride in making a difference and once worked with a child who was struggling with spelling. Lewis gave the student three words to spell and told him he would get a prize if he could spell them right. The student got every word right, although he was so determined to memorize the words Lewis gave him, he forgot to study the other words for his test that week.

"It shows you how much these kids look up to the guys and hang on every word," Baxter said. "They are an awesome and humble group of guys. They are young men with the kind of exemplary character that you want every child to be around."

The students not only had a chance to see the Oilers in school every week but they also attended games and swarmed to the players after the game to get autographs.

As much as the Oilers inspired the students, the players benefited just as much from the experience. It's easy to be seduced by the hype that comes with success. Helping out school students helped keep the players humble. "Sometimes we get so wrapped up in the next practice or the next game, and what happens to a lot of athletes is that they miss out on the reality of life," Ernst said. "They learn that away from the wins and losses, and away from basketball, they have it pretty good in life. I like it that our players do it because it keeps them grounded."

Bostic agreed.

"It shows you there is more to life than just basketball," Bostic said. "Being in this situation makes you want to do even more to help others."

As much as Bostic, Lewis and the other Oilers enjoyed the experience of giving back, they were also thrilled about heading back to the NCAA tournament, only this time; the expectations were as high as they had ever been at Findlay.

41 NCAA TOURNAMENT OPENER: GRAND VALLEY STATE

Findlay's opponent in the opening round of the NCAA tournament was a familiar one. Grand Valley State earned the eighth seed, setting up one final battle between the Oilers and Lakers. Coaches and players tell me all the time how tough it is to beat an opponent three times but I'm not sure what the degree of difficulty is in trying to beat a team four times. One thing was for certain. The bag of secrets was empty for both teams heading into Saturday night's regional quarterfinal showdown.

"It's difficult to find something they are going to be unfamiliar with and they are in the same position as us," Niekamp said, in practice that week. "We know each other as well as we know ourselves."

One of Wesley's assistant coaches joked after the GLIAC tournament he hoped the Lakers wouldn't have to play the Oilers in the first round. The Lakers didn't get their wish but making it into the NCAA tournament with a 21-9 record was the bright side of the situation.

"Going toward the end of the season, we weren't sure if we were even going to get into the tournament but our guys played hard and gave a great effort the last week of the season," Wesley said. "Findlay has a great program and you have to be at your best when you play them. We're looking forward to the opportunity in front of us."

If the Oilers were going to hold off the Lakers, they would need to be much better offensively than they were in the tournament championship game. Bostic, named the Midwest Region Player of the year on the eve of the tourney, talked about the emphasis the Oilers had put on cleaning up mistakes.

"Really, we have spent a lot of time watching film and working on the little things in practice," said Bostic, who was averaging 17.9 points and 6.3 rebounds per game. "We want to learn from our mistakes and execute better this time around."

The Oilers were averaging 79.9 points per outing but had not scored more than 69 in a game against the Lakers during the season. The Lakers were averaging 71.8 points per outing but had scored more than 60 only once against the Oilers in the previous three games.

"We are both good defensive teams but neither has had great success on the offensive end," Niekamp said. "It shows in the stats. Hopefully, we can find a way to get better shots off this time and be more efficient."

Although the Oilers drew a tough matchup, they were thrilled to be playing at home.

"We just have to play our game," said Parker, who was averaging 10.6 points per game and dishing out

4.3 assists per outing entering the NCAA tournament. "We need to work as a team, execute on offense and play hard-nosed defense."

Those had been the recipe for success all season. There was no shortage of motivation for the unbeaten Oilers either.

"We don't need any extra motivation," Parker said. "It's the tournament. It doesn't get any better than that."

Because Findlay was the top seed, it had to play a game during the night session of the tournament. The Oilers chose the first game. A battle with fourth-seeded Southern Indiana awaited the winner. The Screaming Eagles, national champions in 1995 under then head coach Bruce Pearl and the national runner-up in 2003, won their tourney opener with a 78-72 win over Rockhurst earlier in the day.

Another capacity crowd was on hand to watch the Oilers play and the crowd cheered as Hyde swished home a 3-pointer from up top to give Findlay a 5-0 lead. Shots as that were rare in a back-and-forth opening half where the score was tied nine times. Roberts broke one of those ties as he cut through the lane and scored on a layup. He was fouled on the play and his ensuing free throw gave the Oilers a 16-13 lead with eight minutes to play. Evans' jumper tied the game at 18-18 but the Oilers soon lost momentum as the Lakers bullied their way inside for easy shots to push in front 23-18.

Bostic's putback and a layup off a steal by Lewis trimmed the Lakers' lead to 23-22, but with two minutes remaining, the Oilers were down 27-24. Hyde changed that in a hurry as he knocked down a trey to tie the game. The Oilers and Lakers went into halftime tied at 29-29. Findlay knew it needed to create breathing room early in the second half and it did with an 11-2 run. Roberts started it with a layup. Hyde followed with two free throws. Parker scored on a layup and Lewis threw down a dunk. A layup and free throw by Lewis, who was fouled on his shot, put the Oilers in front 40-31. The Lakers failed to make a basket during the run, their only points coming off two free throws. When Hyde hit a 3-pointer with a little over nine minutes to go, he smiled and exchanged high fives with his teammates. The Oilers were in control and on their way to dismantling the Lakers, 66-51. It was the thirty-first win of the year for the Oilers, setting a school record for wins in a season behind 20 points by Bostic, who capped his night with a jumper that put Findlay on top 62-47 with two minutes left. Lewis scored 14 points and pulled down seven rebounds. Hyde nailed three treys and scored 13 points.

"Playing in this tournament is so much fun and I felt so much more comfortable the second time around," Hyde said. "I got some good looks, thanks to my teammates, and I hit my shots."

With one win down in the tourney, Findlay shifted its attention to Southern Indiana, a perennial power in Division II.

42 NCAA TOURNAMENT REGIONAL
SEMIFINAL: SOUTHERN INDIANA

Before any big game, I walk around and take the pulse of the moment, getting a feel for what the fans or other members of the media are thinking about the game. Surprisingly, even though the Oilers were the top-ranked team, several people I chatted with prior to tipoff believed the Screaming Eagles were going to turn the lights out on the Oilers' championship dream. Southern Indiana was ranked No. 19 in the country. The last time the Oilers and Screaming Eagles played was in 2004 when the Oilers were knocked off 75-67 in the semifinal round of the NCAA regional. Southern Indiana certainly had the athletes to keep pace with Findlay and there was no question this would be one of the biggest challenges the Oilers had faced all season.

With a little more than 2,000 fans settled into their seats, it was time for Findlay to battle for a trip to the Sweet 16. Lewis opened the game with a dunk. Two missed 3-pointers later, the Oilers were in a 5-2 hole. They trailed 10-9 before Parker delivered from beyond the arc. Evans hit a trey less than two minutes later and Findlay was in front 15-12. In the first ten minutes of the game, the Oilers and Screaming Eagles were tied four times. Hyde gave Findlay a 25-21 advantage at the midway point of the half. Southern Indiana erased its deficit and pushed in front 27-25. The pace of the game was picking up, and yet, Southern Indiana found a way to stay a step ahead of Findlay. The Screaming Eagles led 30-25 with six minutes to go and the Oilers couldn't afford to let the hole get any deeper.

Bostic wouldn't let it happen. This was the time of the year where National Player of the Year candidates rise to the occasion. The senior leader did just that. He drove into the lane for a layup and hit three free throws as well as the Oilers sliced the Southern Indiana lead to 32-30 with just over four minutes to go in the half. The Oilers took the lead back on a 3-pointer by Hyde and Roberts was fouled as he scored inside. The free throw swished through and the Oilers were up 36-32 with 1:19 to go. The exclamation point on the strong finish to the half was Bostic's layup with thirty seconds left. He was fouled on the shot and punched the air in celebration. The free throw was money in the bank and the Oilers went into halftime with a 41-32 lead. Southern Indiana had been blitzed by a 16-2 run and didn't make a shot from the field in the final four minutes of the half.

Parker and Hyde opened the second half with 3-pointers, and when Lewis delivered a slam dunk off a lob from Bostic with sixteen minutes to go, the Oilers had a 51-44 lead and the Screaming Eagles wanted a timeout as the capacity crowd roared. Southern Indiana players shook their heads in disbelief as their coach, Rick Herdes, tried to settle them down. Jamar Smith, who scored 17 points, hit a jumper out of the timeout to momentarily stop the bleeding, cutting the Findlay lead to 51-46. Back-to-back 3-pointers by Hyde gave the Oilers a 57-46 lead.

Bostic proceeded to score eight straight points, including three on a long-distance shot where he held his hand in the air at the end of the release of the shot and watched the ball rip through the net for a 67-50 Findlay advantage. The shot, Bostic's only 3-pointer of the night, whipped the crowd into a frenzy. You could see it in Bostic's eyes that he had the look of a player who knew he was on his way to the Sweet 16. He finished the game with 25 points. Findlay's lead hit 20 when Lewis came through with another dunk to give the Oilers a 77-57 advantage. The Oilers not only executed their offense to near perfection in the second half, they were downright stingy on defense as well enroute to an 81-59 victory. The Screaming Eagles made only four field goals in the final fifteen minutes of the game. Bostic was overwhelmed with excitement and he talked about why he stopped to admire his 3-pointer, freezing that dagger shot in time.

"I'm a senior and I want to have as much fun as I can," said Bostic, who went 7-of-13 from the field and 10-of-11 from the free-throw line. "Moments like these don't last forever. Before you know it, your career is over."

Bostic wasn't ready for his career to end, nor were the Oilers ready to let their pursuit of a dream come to a close.

"They have a lot of impressive players," Niekamp said. "We know they can score in bunches and we knew we had to do a good job on the defensive end. We didn't give them a lot of good possessions and, on our end; we hit high-percentage shots."

Herdes watched in horror as the Oilers ran his team through the shredder in the second half. He acknowledged after the game that the Oilers were, perhaps, the best team his Screaming Eagles had faced all year, which is saying a lot when you consider how tough the Great Lakes Valley Conference is.

"They are physically tough and mentally tough," Herdes said. "They are definitely a great basketball team. I thought our defensive strategy was sound but they made plays. When you shoot the way they did, you win a lot of games."

Parker had a lot to do with the Oilers' efficiency on the offensive end of the floor. He carved up the Screaming Eagles time and again, either by scoring on easy layups or by kicking the ball out to an open shooter. Parker scored 18 points and dished out seven assists and, as Herdes told me, "Their point guard is a lot better than I thought."

Herdes also praised Hyde, who nailed five treys and lit up the scoreboard for 18 points.

"Nathan Hyde hit terrific shots. He is an unbelievable shooter," Herdes said. "We didn't do a good job of containing him."

The Oilers owned the glass, holding a 31-22 edge in rebounds. Roberts led the way as he pulled down ten rebounds to go along with his seven points.

"Rebounding was a big factor," Niekamp said. "It was so important against a very good rebounding team. I thought we also worked hard to deny their inside players the ball. We stuck with them."

Standing in the way of a trip to the Elite Eight was Bellarmine, the second seed in the region and the 18th-ranked team in the nation. The Knights, who hailed from Louisville and were once ranked as high as No. 2 in the country during the season, defeated Lake Superior State 92-83 in the other semifinal Sunday night. The Oilers, at 32-0, were one step away from a regional title and one step closer to a national championship. The excitement of this tournament was about to go to another level as the Oilers and Knights prepared to square off March 17th, a Tuesday night, in Croy Gymnasium.

Bostic had heard the whispers from outsiders, the people who didn't think Findlay was good enough to win a national championship. He didn't care about what others thought. "The coaches have done a great job of preparing us and we are out to earn respect for our team and our conference."

43 INSTANT CLASSIC

Bostic and Lewis talked often about putting another Elite Eight banner on the wall at Croy Gymnasium and now they were on the verge of doing it, although they had plans to go even further than the 2005 team did. The Oilers had Monday off as there is always a one-day break between the semifinal and final round of the regional. Tuesday arrived soon enough and the Oilers were ready for a showdown with the Knights. It was a warm and sunny St. Patrick's Day afternoon and I arrived at the gym a couple of hours before the opening tip. Lines had already started forming at both entrances of Croy when I got to the gym. The lines included fans who were hopeful they could get their hands on the precious few tickets available for sale at the door. The Oilers were the hottest ticket in town and, because only a handful of tickets were available, a lot of fans had to settle for listening to the game on the radio.

Inside the gymnasium, the atmosphere was nothing I'd ever experienced before. The Findlay students were out in full force and several of the football players went shirtless to the game, covering their chests in body paint. Six of the players each had a letter on his chest that spelled out OILERS. Bellarmine brought its share of fans, too, including its pep band, and most of the fans were wearing white shirts. The two fan bases went back and forth with chants as the Oilers and Knights warmed up. Music boomed through the gymnasium and the feeling in the air was that this game was going to live up to the hype.

As the ball was tipped into the air, the sell-out crowd roared and Bostic converted on the Oilers' first possession, drilling a jumper for a 2-0 lead. Bellarmine opted to attack inside early and scored its first eight points off layups to push in front 8-4. Bostic, who had waited for this moment since the loss in the regional final to Grand Valley a year earlier, responded with a jumper, making it clear he was ready to put on a show. With the Knights up 11-7, Hyde knocked down a 3-pointer. Bostic's 3-pointer tied the game at 13-13 before Evans drilled a trey to give the Oilers a 16-13 lead, with a little over eleven minutes left in the first half. The lead was Findlay's first since Bostic's jumper in the opening minute. Roberts stretched the lead to 18-13 and it appeared the Oilers were about to get on a roll as they had done so many times before during the season. The Knights answered, responding with a 5-0 run that tied the score at 18-18. Back-to-back shots by Bostic gave the Oilers a 22-18 advantage before Evans and Parker stepped up and knocked down 3-pointers as the Oilers surged in front 28-20. The pace of the game was maddening, the game shaping up to be everything a championship battle should be.

The Knights refused to back down and got within two at 29-27 with five minutes left. Lewis jolted the Knights with a dunk for a 31-27 advantage before Laflin connected on a jumper with three minutes to go to put the Oilers on top 33-29. When Lewis fired up the crowd with another dunk with 1:14 left, the Oilers were holding onto a 38-33 lead. The lead didn't last as Bellarmine finished the half strong to tie the score at 38-38 at the half. Twenty minutes was all that stood between the Oilers and a trip to the Elite Eight in Springfield, Mass. If the Oilers were going to make it happen, it was going to take their best second half of the season.

With the Oilers struggling to get shots to fall, Bellarmine cashed in and went in front 50-46 after Justin Benedetti, one of the Knights' most versatile scoring threats, nailed a 3-pointer with just over 13 minutes to go in the game. Two free throws by Nick Holmes stretched the Bellarmine lead to 52-46. Fears of an upset were real, and as the clock rolled to the eight-minute mark of the second half, the Oilers trailed 58-54. Giving up wasn't an option. Evans drilled a 3-pointer from the corner and cut the Knights' lead to 58-57. Another 3-pointer by Evans a couple of minutes later cut the Knights' lead to 63-61. Hyde's jumper tied the game at 63-63 with 5:34 remaining.

Finally, with 4:22 left, the Oilers took their first lead of the second half, slipping in front 66-65 as Hyde buried a 3-pointer while the crowd cheered. Bellarmine responded and went back on top 67-66 but Bostic took the ball hard to the basket and scored on a layup while drawing a foul. His free throw was good as well and the Oilers led 69-67. Bostic missed out on a chance to put the Oilers in front by four as his jumper bounced off the rim and the Knights soon tied the game at 69-69 as the clock approached two minutes. Evans and Hyde each took a turn trying to break a 71-71 tie. Both of their 3-point attempts only found the rim. A layup by Lewis tied the game at 73-73. With the Oilers trailing 75-73 with under thirty seconds left in an intense and exciting game, Bostic stepped up and hit one of the biggest shots of his life, pulling up from 3-point range and swishing home a trey that gave the Oilers a 76-75 lead with ten seconds left. Bellarmine would have the basketball back with one final opportunity to pull off the upset. Chartrael Hall decided to take matters into his own hands for the Knights. He quickly pushed the ball up the floor and drove to the basket. He didn't score but did draw a foul with six seconds left. Even if Hall did make both shots, the Oilers would only be down one and have time to get a shot off for the win.

The problem is end-of-game situations are always chaotic, and even the most well-designed plays aren't guaranteed to work. Before Hall settled in at the line to attempt his free throws, the football players who were sitting behind the basket on the other end of the floor ran down the sideline and stood in front of the bleachers behind the basket Hall was shooting at. They started waving their hands and cheering. It was a great idea, and the thing of it is, it worked. Hall was rattled and the ball on his first free-throw attempt bounced off the rim. The best the Knights could do at that point was tie the game and hope for overtime.

Hall did make the second free throw. The Oilers tried to win the game in regulation. A layup attempt by Parker came up short and Lewis ran out of time to tip the miss in for the win.

The important thing was the Oilers had new life and the belief was they wouldn't let the opportunity go to waste in overtime. Bostic tied the game at 78-78 on two free throws with four minutes left in overtime and Roberts gave the Oilers an 80-78 lead thirty seconds later. Bostic rose to the occasion with 2:28 left as he knocked down a clutch 3-pointer that put the Oilers in front 83-79. Bostic's jumper stretched the Findlay lead to 85-81. The Knights refused to give up, however, and closed the gap to 85-84 after Andrew Patterson nailed a 3-pointer with 1:09 left in the extra session. Parker made one of the biggest plays of the overtime moments later. With the Oilers clinging to an 85-84 lead, he poked the ball out of the hands of Hall, who was trying to post up and get to the basket for an easy shot. As the ball bounced out of bounds, Parker got to it and threw it back in. The ball bounced off the legs of Hall and went out of bounds. The possession was awarded to the Oilers.

Evans was fouled on the other end and hit two free throws, putting the Oilers in front 87-84 with thirteen seconds left. Bellarmine wasn't done yet and opted to run a play for Benedetti. The play was designed to get him a look from the 3-point line. He pulled up for his shot, and it initially looked like it was a 3-pointer as it ripped through the net. The officials, however, with the courtesy of replay provided by the local television crew doing the game, ruled the shot was only worth two. The Knights still trailed by one. The television monitor was right next to me at the press table. I took a look at it as the officials looked things over. It was clear the shot was not a 3-pointer. The officials got the call right, even if Bellarmine did believe otherwise. The team was furious, as were its fans, and no matter how hard head coach Scott Davenport pleaded with the refs, his words fell on deaf ears.

Hyde finished off the game with a pair of free throws and the Oilers erupted in celebration as their riveting 89-86 win over the Knights catapulted them into the Elite Eight. The players, now three wins away from a national title, were mobbed in the middle of the court by the fans and they savored the thrill of accomplishing another goal. Bostic paved the way. He was locked into a zone all night and wasn't going to let the Oilers lose as he scored a career-high 37 points. Even today, I still tell people it was the greatest individual performance I have ever witnessed in a basketball game. Bostic scored seven of his points in overtime and willed the Oilers to a win.

"This feels good," Bostic said, as he spoke over the music playing inside the gym. "We have worked so hard through the preseason and the season itself. This is why we did all of that work."

Bostic was named the MVP of the regional as he hit on eleven of his sixteen attempts from the field. He drilled four 3-pointers to help punctuate his performance. Lewis only scored six points but played a pivotal role defensively. I asked him if he was ever concerned over the course of the game that the Oilers would fall short of a victory. His response was an instant classic as far as quotes are concerned.

"We're in Croy, baby. We don't lose in Croy," Lewis said. "We weren't going to lose this game.

Seriously, we felt like we had the momentum and that we would get the job done."

The Oilers shot 53.7 percent from the field in the back-and-forth battle with the Knights. Bellarmine shot the ball better, connecting on 57.4 percent of its shots. Holmes and Hall each scored 19 points. Evans proved to be an X-factor for the Oilers, who narrowly avoided a replay of 2007 when their dream season was ruined by Northern Kentucky in a regional semifinal at Croy. Evans had ice water in his veins as he hit four 3-pointers. He only missed one time from beyond the arc. Evans was a sophomore in 2007 and never forgot that gut-wrenching moment.

"We were sophomores and I remember the look in the eyes of the seniors," Evans said. "Everyone felt so bad for them. We didn't want our season to end like that."

Davenport, who would guide the Knights to the national title in 2011, did have to deal with the end to his team's season. "Our kids played as hard as they could tonight," Davenport said. "I wouldn't have changed anything. We gave it our all against the No. 1 team in the nation and came up a little short."

The game was an instant classic. Both teams left everything they had on the floor as they battled for the regional title in, arguably, the toughest region in the country. Niekamp could not have been prouder of his Oilers and their ability to find a way to win with a crazy amount of pressure on their shoulders.

"Both teams laid it on the line tonight," Niekamp said after the game. "There were stretches where they couldn't stop us and we couldn't stop them. The fans got their money's worth for a championship game.

Right now, we want to savor this and then we'll get back to work."

Springfield was the next stop for the Oilers. The stage was set for a showdown between the top two teams in the nation on March 25th at the MassMutual Center in downtown Springfield. C.W. Post out of New York was also unbeaten at 30-0 and was ranked No. 2 in the country. One very good basketball team was going to be done playing after one night at the Elite Eight. The Oilers, of course, were the favorite. Ranked No. 1 all year, the Oilers worked hard for a shot at the title, and nothing less than a championship would do, especially for a senior class led by Bostic and Lewis.

"It feels good to win this regional, but we aren't done yet," Bostic said. "We are going to Springfield with the mindset that we can win it all."

44 REMEMBERING JAVONTE

More than a half decade later, the memories of Clanton were still vivid for Bostic and, in some ways, the death of his friend affected him more now than it did in 2009. He said there are still moments when he thinks about Clanton and wonders what life would have held for him if he were still alive.

"To be honest, the death of Javonte didn't really affect me at the time," Bostic said. "He was one of my best friends and it hurt to lose him but I was able to go forward and play basketball. I think it hits me a lot more now, like when I'm at home or driving down the road. I think a lot about what might have been for him."

Clanton had a great deal of potential. He was a communications major and a bright student who was in a position to have success outside basketball. Before the start of his junior season, he told his coach that he wanted to have the highest grade point average on the team. He accomplished that goal.

Clanton, though, also had the potential to make a living playing basketball and Bostic couldn't help but wonder what heights Clanton would have soared to as a basketball player.

"I think a lot about what might have been," Bostic said. "He would have been a great player. He was definitely good enough to play at the next level."

As talented as Clanton was as a basketball player, he was a good person as well. His bright smile and his friendliness was what so many of his teammates talked about in news reports following his death. The memory of Clanton has lived on at Aiken, just as it has lived on with Bostic. The school set up a scholarship in his name and Coach Alexander noted whatever player wore No. 22 in the future would have to have the same kind of heart that Clanton played with night in and night out, during his one season with the Pacers. In a game the following January, Aiken was taking on Augusta State at home and, as the final seconds ticked off the clock in a 71-68 victory, the fans chanted No. 22.

Bostic didn't talk much about the tragedy the week it happened and it was a story not many knew about as the Oilers played through the Elite Eight. Bostic did what he knew his friend would have wanted him to, which was to play as determined as he could and has hard as he could in pursuit of a title. With a national championship on the line, Bostic already had enough motivation to play his best in Springfield. The chance to play in honor of Clanton was an added incentive in what would be the biggest week of Bostic's collegiate basketball career.

45 IMPORTANCE OF ROLE PLAYERS

It was safe to say the Oilers weren't going to be happy just playing at the Elite Eight. They expected nothing less than a national championship, and I had even written a blog earlier in the week making the claim that Findlay would win the title, if it played up to its potential. One of the keys to the Oilers' success up to this point was the play of their bench. There was a concern about the strength of the bench because of Sparks' injury. Sparks averaged 6.1 points and 3.9 rebounds per game before getting hurt and was also one of the top defenders on the team, having tallied twenty-nine steals. He was one of those players who was all effort, all of the time. Although Sparks was sidelined, his teammates were inspired to play even harder because of him.

"Tyler's jersey is hanging up in the locker room, and it's a reminder for us to always play hard," Wehri said as the Oilers prepared for their trip to Springfield. "It was terrible to see Sparks go down but myself and the other guys on the bench have stepped up and played even harder."

Wehri always played hard and he and Agunga had done an admirable job of giving Roberts breathers during the game while Evans, Laflin and Coon provided valuable minutes in the backcourt. Without question, the Oilers had star power, particularly in Bostic and Lewis, yet the role players would have to do their jobs, as well, if Findlay was going to come home from Springfield as national champions.

"I think we have seen throughout the tournament how important role players can be," Niekamp said, in an interview before his team headed out for the Elite Eight. "They have been able to come in and maintain the level of intensity our starters play with and have all contributed in different ways."

Laflin had done his part by giving Parker breaks at the point guard position. He was averaging 3.8 points per game and had dished out forty-one assists in thirty-three games. It's not always easy for bench players to accept their role without complaining but Laflin knew, as did his teammates, it was all about doing what was best for the team.

"I know when I get into the game, I just want to provide energy and do whatever I can to help the team," Laflin said, in an interview a few days before the team left for the Elite Eight. "Everyone on the team has accepted his role and has bought into what we are trying to accomplish."

Part of what made the Oilers' bench successful was those players coming off it were prepared for the rigors of the game-to-game grind because of what they went through in practice.

"It's great having guys like Lee and Josh and Morgan because they have so much experience and are willing to always give pointers," Wehri said. "And when you go up against players who are good in practice, you learn how to step up, too. The experience is something I wouldn't trade for anything in the world."

Niekamp understood his Oilers would need everyone to be at their best to survive three more games. The beauty of having a deep bench was that anyone was capable of stepping up at any given time, which gave the Oilers added confidence as they prepared for their trip.

"Sometimes it's the mystery man that steps up in a tournament game," said Niekamp, who was entering the Elite Eight with a record of 547-174. "He might make a play or two that changes the momentum. You just hope it's one of your guys."

46 PREVIEWING THE ELITE EIGHT

It was unfair that the top two teams in the nation had to square off in the quarterfinal round of the Elite Eight. The brackets were set up in advance, though, and this was the year the Midwest and East region champs were pitted against each other on the first day of the marquee event for NCAA Division II basketball.

Post was under the direction of Tim Cluess, who is now the head coach at Division I Iona, and Cluess had put the Pioneers on an impressive path to success after taking over the program in 2006. His Pioneers were only 19-11 in 2007, but put together a 26-5 campaign in 2008 enroute to winning a second consecutive East Coast Conference championship. The Pioneers were a lot like the Oilers as they played unselfish basketball and had several veteran players capable of rising to the occasion at any given moment, including senior guard Johnathan Schmidt, who was putting up 19.1 points per game. Senior guard, Nick Carter, was averaging 18.1 points per outing and senior guard, Kenny Burkes, was averaging 13.9 points per game. Senior guard, Kevin Spann, owned a scoring average of 11.1 points per outing. As a team, Post was averaging 86.3 points per game and had racked up 605 assists. The Pioneers were allowing 62.8 points per game.

"There is no doubt that our balance has been a huge part of our success," Cluess said. "We are very unselfish and that allows us to get good shots. What I really like about this team is the way we play defense. We really get after it."

Niekamp said his biggest concern with the Pioneers was their offensive attack. "They have very good guards and they are all great shooters," Niekamp said. "They have the ability to beat you off the dribble. They are very quick. It's a difficult offense to defend."

Post had proven in its regional final it was going to be a tough team to put away. The Pioneers trailed 42-24 to Bentley early in the second half of their Sweet 16 showdown before rallying for an 82-76 win. Burkes scored 23 points, including two on a layup that gave Post the lead for good at 64-63 with 6:34 remaining.

"To win a game like that shows just how great the character of this team is," Cluess said. "Our guys never quit fighting. We didn't want our season to end and our seniors stepped up and made sure that it didn't happen."

Bostic talked to me about how impressed he was with the Pioneers. He respected their talent but felt confident he and his teammates would be ready for the next hurdle on their trail to glory.

"We know they are a great basketball team. They

wouldn't be at the Elite eight if they weren't good," Bostic said. "The coaches have done a great job of getting film ready for us to watch and are making sure we understand their strengths and weaknesses. But it's also important that we focus on our end of things, making sure we go out and execute and play our kind of basketball."

Bostic and I caught up on the phone over the weekend before the Elite Eight. He was still dealing with the pain of losing one of his best friends, while trying to enjoy the current moment with his teammates. In a few days, Bostic would be named the Division II National Player of the Year. It was a heck of an honor for a player who was always taught hard work paid off. Bostic was a two-time All-American, the only one in program history and he is still the only player in school history to score at least 1,500 points, grab 700-plus rebounds, dish out 200 assists and tally 200 steals. He was humbled by every accolade and took a great deal of satisfaction in helping the Oilers reach the doorstep of greatness.

"People always talk about how hard work pays off and it's exciting that it has for me," Bostic said, during the interview. "But first I need to thank God because without Him, none of this would be possible. My teammates deserve a lot of credit, too. This National Player of the Year Award is as much for them as it is for me."

It was impressive that even in a time in his life when most would have their faith rattled, Bostic, despite having a friend die tragically, maintained his faith in God. It said a lot about Bostic as a person. Lewis admired what Bostic had accomplished.

"He's the nation's best player and we have all followed his lead," Lewis said. "Being able to play against him in practice every day has made us all better."

Bostic not only gave credit to his teammates but he praised his parents as well. Jerome and Linda Bostic not only offered advice constantly and loved their son dearly but they also did a remarkable job of keeping Bostic humble.

"I can always call them when I need to and they are always there to make sure I don't get a big head about anything," Bostic said. "They point out the good and the bad and my dad, being a former player, is always giving me pointers about basketball."

Bostic entered the Elite Eight with 1,655 points and had pulled down 737 rebounds. His career assist and steal totals were at 268 and 232, respectively. Hanging 37 points on Bellarmine in the regional final highlighted his ability to be a dangerous scorer. It was his third 30-point game of the season but Bostic didn't want to be defined by his scoring ability alone.

"I don't want to be known as just a great scorer," Bostic said. "I feel like I got the National Player of the Year Award because I am a pretty complete player and I always play hard. People clown with me sometimes about being a bruiser, but I like being a physical player."

I asked Bostic about the most memorable moment of his career, at least up to this point—more memories were still left to be made—and he brought up the exhibition win over Ohio State.

"I am from Columbus and I always drove by OSU's arena thinking about how great it would be to play there one day," Bostic said. "To have a chance to beat the Buckeyes in their gym was a sweet experience."

The one memory that could trump the win over the Buckeyes was a national championship. "It would be even better than beating Ohio State," Bostic said. "We feel good about the way this season has gone and it would be an unbelievable feeling if we could win a championship."

Bostic and his senior teammates always believed playing for a national championship was a realistic goal. Seeing a banner from the 2005 Elite Eight hanging on the wall in Croy was a reminder of the high standards of the program and it pushed the Oilers to want to finish the job this time. "You can't ever predict the future, but we did feel like we had a good group of players coming in when I was a freshman," Bostic said. "I always told them we were going to put an Elite Eight banner up on the wall like the 2004-05 team did."

Roberts had the same dream and, as he got set for the biggest week of his career, he reflected on his decision to come to Findlay. "When I was a senior in high school, I remember thinking how great it would be to play for a program as successful as Findlay. It was one of the reasons I signed here," Roberts said. "I couldn't have asked for a better place to play basketball."

As talented as the five seniors were, egos were never an issue. All five cared about what was best for the team. "They have gelled so well together and their skills complement each other," Ernst said. "They are also unselfish players by heart, and that willingness to work as a team is one of the reasons we have had this kind of season."

No one on the Oilers took the success for granted and, while they were, no doubt, playing for themselves, they were also playing for past Findlay teams that helped blaze the trail for the 2008-09 team. This was for the Oilers who took Kentucky Wesleyan right down to the wire in 2002; it was for the Oilers who went to the Elite Eight in 2005 and for the Oilers of 2007, who walked off the floor in the regional with tears in their eyes after being stunned by Northern Kentucky.

"When we were cutting down the nets after the regional, 2005 Elite Eight team member Tyson McGlaughlin told us; it's about time we got to the Elite Eight," Roberts said. "He told us to go all the way this time."

Bostic said he and his teammates had been flooded with text messages from former players since winning the regional. "We get text messages all of the time from alumni telling us they are supporting the team," Bostic said. "We feel like we are not only playing for ourselves, but we are playing for the teams that came before us."

47 HYPE REACHES ITS PEAK

I left for Springfield late Monday and drove through the night. As morning arrived in the East, I crossed into Massachusetts and was ready to hit the ground running with coverage of the Oilers at the Elite Eight. After taking some time to rest at the hotel, I headed over to the arena late Tuesday afternoon to talk with the Oilers, after their practice at the MassMutual Center. A couple of television camera crews were on hand to do interviews, as well, while photographers were busy testing the lighting in the arena. All of it added to the big-time feel of the three-day event. The Oilers and Pioneers were set to battle in the first No. 1 vs. No. 2 matchup since 2007 when Winona State took on Bentley. That game was also a national quarterfinal. Winona State won 64-51 but would lose the national championship game against Barton, which got 10 points from Anthony Atkinson in the final minute, the final two on a game-winning layup off a steal by Atkinson as time expired. As Lewis came off the floor after practice, I approached him to talk about finally being in Springfield and playing in a battle of unbeatens right out of the gate.

"It's exciting to be part of a game like this," Lewis said. "There is a lot of publicity and exposure around this game. Hopefully, we come out on top."

Lewis talked about the video session he and his teammates sat through earlier in the day, along with the scouting report they went over. "We know we have to play smart and disciplined on defense," Lewis told me. "We also feel like we can create matchup problems for them. Both teams look good on paper. It comes down to who can execute."

Carter, one of the stars of Post, echoed those thoughts during an interview I had with him after the team's practice. Carter also talked about the reality of the situation facing both teams.

"We are both undefeated but, unfortunately, one team is going to have to leave with a loss," Carter said. "It should be a great game."

Part of handling the hype of a big-time event is dealing with the distractions and the agenda the NCAA has set up for teams. The Oilers arrived by air Monday and spent part of their time during the first two days doing community service work and paying a visit to the Naismith Memorial Basketball Hall of Fame, which was only a few blocks away from the arena.

"We've had a lot of preliminary things to do and had a chance to see the pro basketball hall of fame. That was a neat experience," Niekamp said, during an interview after his team's 55-minute practice in the arena. "We are anxious to start playing. We have a mature team that has done a good job of handling this experience, which is what you expect from a group of veterans."

Lewis felt good about how ready the Oilers were for the challenges ahead and excited about making a four-year dream come true. "We used to talk as freshmen about how good we could be as seniors," Lewis said. "It's amazing how far we have come. We definitely have high expectations for this week."

48 BATTLE OF UNBEATENS

Wednesday morning arrived and the sun was shining. I planned on checking out the other three games of the tournament as the Oilers weren't scheduled to play until the end of the night. Four games in one day is a basketball junkie's dream. I was ready for my fix.

Augusta State of Georgia and Christian Brothers of Tennessee opened the day. The Jaguars of Augusta were ranked fourth in the nation, making their second straight Elite Eight trip. The Buccaneers were No. 15 in the country and making their first ever trip, which would be short-lived as Augusta State, the national runner-up a year earlier, held off Christian Brothers 70-62. In the second game, unranked Cal Poly Pomona took on No. 12 Southwest Minnesota State. The Broncos were the only unranked team here at the Elite Eight and were in it for the first time since 2005. The Mustangs were making their first trip since 2001. Cal Poly played nothing like an unranked team and stunned Southwest Minnesota 74-69 to set up a semifinal battle with Augusta State Thursday.

Gannon, a former rival of the Oilers in the GLIAC before going to the Pennsylvania State Athletic Conference after the 2007-08 season, took on Central Missouri in the third game. The Golden Knights were ranked fifth and in the Elite Eight for the first time since 1990. The sixth-ranked Mules were making their fourth appearance, including their first since 2007. I was pulling for Gannon because I was hoping to see the Oilers and Golden Knights go at it one more time. They had played some classics in the past as GLIAC foes. Central Missouri ruined the possibility of another one with an 86-77 win.

With the 8:30 p.m. tip-off closing in, it was time for the Oilers take center stage. They had one of the larger followings at the Elite Eight as music rumbled through the arena while the two teams warmed up. I settled into my seat along press row. My seat was directly across from the Findlay bench. The Oilers were supposed to be the home team but their white jerseys were ruined by body paint when the football players mobbed the Oilers, during their regional championship celebration in Croy. So Findlay would have to wear its black jerseys. Parker started the game with a 3-pointer and it sparked an 8-0 run to open the game. Roberts threw down a dunk and Parker drilled another trey as Findlay took control. Parker played a huge role early on, which wasn't surprising considering his knack for thriving in big games. His layup with sixteen minutes left stretched the Findlay lead to 10-5. His 3-pointer a couple of minutes later gave the Oilers a 15-8 lead. The lead wouldn't last. When Carter pulled up from 3-point land with just over twelve minutes to go, the Pioneers completed a rally and were on top 18-17. Agunga tied the score at

18 with his third free throw of the game.

Schmidt hit from the outside for a 21-18 lead and he connected again from long distance a minute later, as the Pioneers extended their advantage to 26-19. Schmidt wasn't done yet and his third trey of the game gave Post a 33-24 lead with seven minutes to go. A 3-pointer by Carter pushed the Post lead to 36-24. The pressure was on the Oilers to respond. Carter's trey, the fifth of the game for Post, put the Pioneers in front 41-28. What saved the Oilers from disaster was a 7-2 run they went on to close the half. Roberts hit two free throws, Bostic came up with a steal and layup and Parker worked himself open for a 3-pointer at the buzzer as the Oilers went into halftime down 45-37. The Pioneers were lights out in the first half. They made nine 3-pointers on eighteen attempts. Parker did what he could to keep the Oilers within striking distance, as he scored 16 in the first half. Findlay was down but not out.

Bostic opened the second half with a jumper, before the Pioneers responded with a 3-pointer by Schmidt. It was the last shot the Pioneers would make over the next five minutes as the Oilers turned up the heat on defense and opened up a window of opportunity. Roberts scored on a layup, Parker hit a 3-pointer and Roberts threw down a dunk, as the Oilers started to get on a roll. Bostic followed with a jumper and the Oilers and Pioneers were tied at 48-48 with just over sixteen minutes left. Spann's 3-pointer broke the tie. Bostic got the Oilers within one again as he drew a foul, while knocking down a jumper. He didn't make the free throw but Hyde gave the Oilers a 52-51 lead after he hit a jumper. It was back-and-forth from there, as neither team could grab the momentum. Findlay trailed 67-62 with eight minutes left. Evans provided a sliver of hope for a victory when he buried a 3-pointer. A shot by Lewis moments later cut the Post lead to 69-67. A little over five minutes were still on the clock and the tension was building. That is when Roberts took over for the Oilers. It's interesting Roberts would be the player to do it because, in the media room at the regional, a sports information director from another school told me the Oilers would fall short of their title quest because Roberts wasn't good enough at the center position to help Findlay win a championship.

Roberts was ready for this moment, ignoring the pressure of it and playing like the veteran he was, scoring on back-to-back layups and hitting a jumper to give the Oilers a 73-69 lead.

Post rallied and took a 74-73 lead with 1:14 to play as Schmidt scored on a layup and drew a foul. He hit the ensuing free throw to put the Pioneers back on top. Roberts answered with a three-point play of his own, taking the ball to the basket and scoring on a layup. He drew contact and hit a free throw to give the Oilers a 76-74 advantage with forty-five seconds to play. Lewis managed to split two free throws with thirty-one seconds left, as the Oilers pushed their lead to 77-74. Spann answered with a trey to tie the game at 77-77 with nineteen seconds left. The Oilers were unable to come up with a game-winning shot and, for the second consecutive game, they were headed to overtime. Roberts struck first in overtime, as he drove into the lane and scored for a 79-77 lead. Burkes tied the game with a layup of his own but those would be the only points Post would score in the extra session. Evans broke the final tie of the game with two free throws and the Oilers survived, winning the thriller 89-79. Roberts did his part to silence the doubters, establishing himself as a force in the paint and scoring 23 points, a career high, with 11 of those points coming down the stretch of a pressure-packed game. Roberts also grabbed seven rebounds.

"We didn't want to go home," Roberts said, as he spoke into the microphone in the media room. "My teammates did a great job of finding me open on back-cuts and post moves. Fortunately, my shots went in."

The way Post played defense opened the door for Roberts to shine. The Pioneers put a lot of attention on the Oilers' perimeter shooters, forcing the Oilers to look inside for offense. Roberts was there to deliver.

"I thought the play of Lee was huge," Niekamp said, in the press conference. "I think the thing that gets lost about Post is how much pressure they put on the perimeter. We were fortunate to get Lee inside and he was able to make plays and give us confidence."

Cluess was crushed in the wake of the loss. His team fell despite 17 points from Schmidt.

"Roberts did a tremendous job getting inside for them. It just seemed like the shots wouldn't go down even though we had good looks," Cluess said. "They mixed up their zones and made it difficult for us to shoot as well as we did in the first half."

Post shot 45.6 percent from the floor and made fourteen 3-pointers. On a lot of nights, that effort would be good enough for a win. Against the Oilers, it wasn't. The Oilers shot 54.1 percent from the field and Parker led the way with 19 points. Bostic scored 18 points, while Evans finished with 12. Lewis added 11 points. Although their victory hopes looked dim at times, particularly at the half, the Oilers never felt like a dead-team walking.

"It's never fun to be down at the half but we never had the feeling we were out of it," Bostic said, after the game. "We kept our heads up, kept our composure and found a way to win."

Bostic and the Oilers were in the very same position in the Sweet 16; they needed to rally against the Knights. The experience paid off for them against the Pioneers.

"This game was much like our regional championship," Niekamp said. "I thought Post gave a tremendous effort. They are so tough to guard and they shoot the 3-pointer so well. I give our guys a lot of credit for keeping their composure and hanging on. We are thrilled to be moving on."

Worn down from the energy spent against Post, the Oilers had less than twenty-four hours to get rested and ready for a national semifinal game against Central Missouri.

49 SECURING A DATE WITH DESTINY

One half of the championship game for Saturday was set by the time the Oilers took the floor Thursday night for its showdown with Central Missouri. Cal Poly opened the night by knocking off a nationally ranked opponent for the second straight night, dropping Augusta State 74-70. The Broncos had obviously been under-rated and were now in a position to win their program's first national title. The Oilers were still alive in their quest to win the program's first national championship as well and, as they ran out of their locker room the Findlay fans stood and cheered. The Oiler fans filled up an entire section of bleachers in the lower level of the arena behind the team's bench. Central Missouri had brought a strong following as well and was hoping to move one step closer to its first championship since winning it all in 1984 in Springfield. The total attendance for the game was announced at 2,442.

Bostic gave the Oilers a quick 2-0 lead but the Mules pulled in front 5-2 after D'Andre Byrd scored on a layup. He was fouled on the shot and hit a free throw to give the Mules a 3-point lead. Findlay trailed 12-8 with fourteen minutes left before Parker came through with a 3-pointer that sliced the Central Missouri lead to one. Bostic's two free throws gave the Oilers their first lead since the opening minute as they went in front 13-12. Just like Post a night earlier, Central Missouri took control as the first half wore on. Two straight shots by Sanijay Watts gave the Mules a 16-13 advantage. When Byrd drained a 3-pointer with under seven minutes left in the half, the Mules had their biggest lead of the night at 27-18. Bostic scored on a putback to pull the Oilers within seven at 27-20. His basket was the last field goal Findlay would make over the final five minutes of the half. Seven free throws, however, kept Findlay within striking distance. It also helped that the Mules struggled to shoot late in the half as they made only one field during the stretch. Findlay trailed 32-27 at halftime and, for the second straight night, was on the verge of a disappointing ending to a spectacular season.

The Oilers came out inspired early in the second half, attacking the basket to generate offense. Roberts scored on a layup and Lewis tipped in a missed shot and threw down a dunk as the Oilers pulled even with the Mules at 35-35. Central Missouri responded and went in front 44-37 after a huge trey by Tremaine Luellen, with a little over fourteen minutes to go. No matter what the Oilers did, they couldn't steal the momentum and time was running out to do it. At the midway point of the second half, Central Missouri was up 50-43. Through the first ten minutes of the half, the Oilers didn't make a shot on the perimeter.

If they were going to battle back and win, they would need to start making shots from the outside. Enter Evans. The 3-point sharp-shooter delivered when the Oilers needed him most. His first trey with nine minutes left cut the Mules' lead to 50-46. His second one closed the gap to 53-49. Laflin drilled a trey moments later to trim the Mules' lead to 53-52. Evans capped the comeback with a jumper as Findlay pushed ahead 54-53 in a national semifinal that was shaping up to be an instant classic.

Bostic made one of the biggest plays of the game, when he came up with a steal and knocked down a jumper on the other end, tying the score at 56-56, with a little over five minutes to go. Bostic hit another jumper seconds later and the Oilers were back on top at 58-56. Lewis broke a 58-58 tie, as he knocked down a shot before Roberts made a clutch play with 3:38 to go, when he grabbed an offensive rebound and drew contact, as he came down with the ball. He went to the line and was money in the moment, hitting two free throws to give Findlay a 62-58 lead. Watts wasn't going to let the Oilers run away with the game. He scored on a layup and got Lewis to foul him on the way up for the shot. The play was a double whammy for the Oilers. Not only did the Mules score but Lewis picked up his fifth foul.

One of Findlay's most important players, a player who had overcome so much to get to this point, was going to have to watch the final three minutes from the bench. I wasn't sure if the Oilers could pull this out without Lewis on the floor in crunch time. Lewis sat on the bench and prayed this wouldn't be how his career ended. He threw a towel to the floor that had been placed on his shoulders by the trainer and sat on the edge of his chair, hoping for the best. Watts delivered a huge blow to those hopes when he nailed a 3-pointer to put the Mules up 63-62. The Oilers couldn't answer, turning the ball over while Central Missouri scored again on a tip-in by Joe Young that gave the Mules a 65-62 edge with less than two minutes left.

Bostic gave the Oilers a glimmer of hope, when he split a pair of free throws to cut the Central Missouri lead to 65-63 with 1:39 left. The Mules had a chance to get the lead back to four but missed a shot with fifty-five seconds to play, leaving the door open for the Oilers to capitalize. Findlay stayed calm even as the pressure rose and Parker lined up in the corner near the Findlay bench and pierced the hearts of the Mules with a dagger 3-pointer. The Findlay fans erupted into a frenzy and the Oilers were now up 66-65 and forty-one seconds away from a trip to the championship game. Central Missouri had no answer. Hyde split two free throws with 13 seconds left and Bostic rebounded a last-gasp shot by the Mules as the Oilers held on for a heart-stopping 67-65 victory. Hyde scored only 5 points but his fifth point was the one that helped seal the deal. I asked him about being at the line in a situation where he needed to make at least one shot. He told me he relished the opportunity.

"That is the position I want to be in," Hyde said. "I only hit one but it feels good to move on. It's a little unreal right now."

It would have been easy for the Oilers to fold up shop and fall short. Once again, the Oilers put that heart of a champion on display. "I think we showed our resiliency in the first half when we didn't let the game get out of hand," Niekamp said, with a look of relief on his face as he talked during a postgame press conference. "We had a hard time running our offense because of the things they were doing against us on defense. We kept it in range and kept grinding."

Grinding was indeed the appropriate word. The Oilers were worn down, their muscles aching from the wear and tear of a long season. They had been given an opponent's best shot one more time and despite playing the late game for a second straight night, they survived. So often teams chasing championships get swallowed up by the pressure, suffer a bad break or simply have a bad night; yet the Oilers had proven how special they were, having survived the pitfalls existing on the road to a title. They did it while maintaining the No. 1 ranking. That they were able to find a way to beat the Mules highlighted the determination of the Oilers.

"There is no quit in us," said Bostic, who scored 19 points despite battling cramps in his legs and a little over a week removed from the death of a close friend. "We are going to fight until the end and I thank God we are still playing. It was a deep relief to get out of this game with a win. We are so close now to what we have been playing for all year."

No one was more relieved than Lewis, who finished with 16 points despite fouling out.

"It was tough to foul out but I guess it was a good call," said Lewis, who also grabbed eleven rebounds. "My teammates told me this wasn't going to be my last game. We had big-time players hit big-time shots."

Central Missouri head coach Kim Anderson, once an assistant under Norm Stewart at Missouri and now the head coach of the Tigers, could only tip his hat to the Oilers. His team played its heart out for forty minutes and Watts scored 18 points. In the end, it wasn't enough.

"They are No. 1 for a reason," said Anderson, who led the Mules to a national championship in 2014. "I thought Findlay executed a little better than we did in the second half. Our team left it all on the floor. I'm proud of them but Findlay was the better team tonight and deserved to win."

The Oilers, set to play the Broncos in a 1 o'clock, national final on CBS, won because they did play as a team, especially late when Lewis was on the bench.

"It's nice when you can count on your teammates," Lewis said. "We are blessed we still have one more game to play."

As the Oilers walked out of the arena, the clock pushing toward midnight in the Eastern time zone, I could tell the players were feeling the effects of playing the late game on back-to-back nights. Several players, including Bostic, were battling soreness in their legs. They were fortunate they would have an off day on Friday to rest up a bit because they were certainly going to need all the rest they could get before Saturday. Inside the arena, "Don't Stop Believing" by Journey played over the speakers. As I wrapped up my game story and prepared to call it a night, I couldn't hold the back the excitement of knowing I was less than forty-eight hours away from covering my first national title game. I poured so much effort into covering this season to the best of my ability and hoped all season for this opportunity. The Oilers couldn't wait for the opportunity either. A date with destiny awaited the No. 1 team in the land.

50 ON THE DOORSTEP OF GREATNESS

Friday was the scheduled off day of the Elite Eight but there was a time in the history of this tournament when teams didn't get a break in between the semifinals and championship game. One game nearly two decades earlier changed everything. It was the 1993 Final Four showdown between Troy State and Southern New Hampshire at the Springfield Civic Center. Troy State made 23 3-pointers in the game and still needed every second of regulation to hold on for a 126-123 victory. While Troy State was able to shine from beyond the arc, Southern New Hampshire scored 100 of its points in the paint. The Spartans were exhausted and didn't return to their team hotel until after midnight. They would have little time to prepare for the title game, which was set to be played later that day against Cal State Bakersfield. Troy State, not surprisingly, had little left in the tank for the championship game and fell 85-72 to unbeaten Bakersfield. The NCAA changed the format the next year so that teams would have an off day, which, I believe, worked in the Oilers' favor.

Findlay did everything it could to take advantage of the situation, canceling its pre-championship game press conference to get a little extra time to relax before Saturday. The entire Friday, however, would not be filled with relaxation time. The Oilers had to film promos for CBS for the game broadcast and, also, had an afternoon scouting report session to attend, inside the team hotel in downtown Springfield.

I spent the day at the Naismith Memorial Basketball Hall of Fame, which provided an amazing look at how the game has grown over the years. So much history is inside the building on West Columbus Avenue, from jerseys worn by some of the game's greatest players to signed basketballs. There is even a basketball court that offers visitors an opportunity to shoot into peach baskets. It was a great way to kill time on a warm spring afternoon but, soon enough, it was time to head over to the hotel for interviews. As I came off the elevator on the sixth floor of the Marriott, I noticed there were a few other media members waiting around, including a radio reporter from Westwood One, the national radio station carrying the game. We started up a conversation and he asked me if I would answer a few questions for him about Findlay. He asked me about Bostic, about the journey this team had taken to get to 35-0 and also threw out a great question about Lewis and his role on the team. I told him Lewis was the 'X-Factor' and he seemed to like that answer. I thought it was an appropriate response because, while Lewis didn't get the attention Bostic did, there is no way the Oilers get this far without Lewis.

Soon enough, the Oilers emerged from their team meeting in a conference room and they had the look of a team ready for this journey to end. The Oilers handled the burden of being the No. 1 team in impressive fashion but, I could tell, they were ready to have that weight come off their shoulders and raise the trophy they had been chasing all season. The Oilers were the favorite to win the national championship and focused on living up to that expectation.

"One game at a time—that has been our solution all year," said Bostic, speaking in the same confident tone he had used in interviews all season. "It's a bigger stage but we have the same mindset we've had all year. We are going out to get the job done."

Lewis had similar thoughts. He believed the Oilers had come too far and knew that if this Findlay team wanted to be remembered forever, it had to win. "We are past the pressure and the hype. We're just ready to go out and take care of business," said Lewis, who was coming off his sixth double-double effort of the year. "We have come so far but we know it doesn't mean a thing without the ring."

For Hyde, this run to the title game was extra special because he was a local kid, having played high school basketball in Findlay. "I'm so excited," said Hyde, who led the team in 3-pointers with 75. "I am very thankful for this opportunity. It goes to show you that hard work does pay off. I couldn't have asked for a better situation to be in."

Wehri said he and his teammates had been thinking about winning a championship all season and yet the pursuit of their ultimate dream had not prevented them from staying focused on each challenge along the way. "Playing for a national championship has been in the back of our minds all year," Wehri said, "but we have stayed so focused on taking it one game at a time. This has been an unbelievable experience. I wouldn't trade it for anything in the world."

Niekamp was the mastermind of this magical ride. The coach who made winning a habit throughout his career, made an interesting point about his team's approach to the championship game, as we talked on Friday afternoon. He understood this was more than just another game still he didn't want his team focusing as much on the possibility of a title as he did on them simply being ready to play. "I don't think we are in the mode of thinking national championship," Niekamp said. "We are focused on our opponent, figuring out matchups, going over scouting reports and just preparing our players the best we can so they are in the best situation possible on Saturday."

Cal Poly, at 27-5, wasn't going to be a pushover. The Broncos embraced being the underdog the same way the Oilers embraced the role of being the team to beat. The Broncos were in their third Elite Eight in seven years. Cal Poly went into the West Regional as the third seed after earning a share of the California Collegiate Athletic Association title and were going into the championship game hoping to become the first unranked team to win a title since 1979 when North Alabama defeated Wisconsin-Green Bay 64-50. Head coach Greg Kamansky was in his ninth season at Cal Poly and had won 176 games. He had the utmost confidence in his team to pull off the upset. After all, not only did Cal Poly beat two ranked teams in Springfield, it had beaten third-ranked BYU-Hawaii 59-58 in the regional title game.

"We've been in tough games all year but our guys show great poise," Kamansky said, in an interview Friday morning. "Obviously, Findlay is a great team but playing for a national title has been our goal all year and hopefully we can give ourselves a chance to win."

Larry Gordon, a senior forward and the heart and soul of the Broncos, talked to me about why his team had been successful and why it was good enough to spoil the Oilers' unbeaten season. "Heart. Point blank. That's what it's all about," Gordon said. "We have shown a lot of heart all year and we are thrilled about having the chance to play for a national title."

Niekamp was impressed with what the Broncos had accomplished, especially here in Springfield after traveling nearly 3,000 miles across the country. Sometimes winning a title is all about getting hot at the right time, and the Broncos were definitely playing their best basketball.

"They seem to be in a zone," Niekamp said. "They are athletic, they defend well in their matchup zone and they do a lot of things that give you problems."

The game between the Oilers and Broncos was going to be a test of wills and, while the Oilers were the lone unbeaten team in the country, they were far from perfect. "While unbeaten, we are not overpowering," Niekamp said. "In terms of consistency, we have been rather inconsistent in some ways; but we have been consistent in that we have always dug down to find a way to win tough games. We have shown more tenacity and we will need that Saturday."

For the seniors, this was it. Those four years seemed to fly by so quickly and the class I always thought had an opportunity to win a title was now forty minutes of basketball away from making its dream come true. You figured the seniors would play the game of their lives knowing there was no tomorrow; but the beauty of the Oilers was anyone was capable of stepping up at any given moment.

"You never know who is going to step up on any given night," Niekamp said. "We've had so many different players contribute, and all of our players have matured a lot and found ways to better themselves as players each week."

Back in Findlay, plans were in place for a watch party in Croy Gymnasium. The pride of Oiler Nation was at an all-time high and Hyde knew the Oilers would be carrying the pride of their city and school on their shoulders along with the pride of the conference and region as well. The Midwest Region had already produced ten national champions. The Oilers were eager to add their name to the list. "So many Findlay people have been telling me how much it means to them that we are playing for a national championship," Hyde said. "We take a lot of pride in playing hard for our fans. Hopefully, we can bring home a title."

51 HEAVYWEIGHT FIGHT FOR THE TITLE

Sunlight sliced through the windows of the MassMutual Center lobby early Saturday morning as fans waited to get into the gym and cheer on their respective teams in the NCAA Division II national championship game. Oiler fans had a dominating presence in the lobby. The football team canceled spring practice and many of the players drove late into the night to be here for a chance to witness history. A lot of the students did the same. With so many Orange-and-Black clad fans hanging out in the lobby nearly an hour before tip-off, I decided to call the MassMutual Center Croy Gymnasium East.

I spent some time talking with fans and even walked around the gym a bit before the fans were allowed in to absorb the atmosphere of the event I was about to cover. I had covered big games in the past but this was the biggest, without a doubt. Arena workers were busy opening up the boxes of national champion t-shirts in one of the hallways and my hope was the Oilers' shirts would get to be worn later that afternoon. The Elite Eight dancers, who performed during timeouts and halftime throughout the tournament, were fine tuning their routine for the game, while the CBS television crew, featuring Tim Brando and Dan Bonner, was busy courtside prepping for their broadcast. As game time approached, I sat in the media room going over notes and then walked through the hallway near the Findlay locker room. I stood outside the locker room for a moment and heard the voices inside growing louder as the players turned up their excitement to another level just before taking the floor for pre-game warmups.

With the music playing and the lights high above the floor as bright as ever, the Oilers burst out of the locker room and through the entrance to the arena as cheers erupted from the Findlay fans. The countdown clock to tip off was on, and in thirty minutes, Findlay and Cal Poly would play for the right to be the last team standing in the 2008-09 season. My seat on press row was the same it had been for the previous two games, directly across from the Findlay bench. Roy Pickerill, the media coordinator for the tournament and a man who has probably forgotten more basketball knowledge than I'll ever know, walked by and asked if I was ready for three million people to see the back of my head. I remember watching the championship game on television as a child and now, all of those years later, I was covering the game live.

Cal Poly struck first on a jumper by Tobias Jahn. Hyde quickly gave the Oilers a 3-2 lead as he buried a 3-pointer with eighteen minutes, seventeen seconds remaining on the clock in the opening half. Bostic followed with a trey of his own and the Oilers pushed their advantage to 6-2. The Oilers played hard on defense early on, forcing a couple of turnovers, and they were patient offensively, holding the ball for the best shot possible.

Five minutes into the action, the Oilers were in front 10-4. Bostic and Roberts both hit short jumpers and Jahn was still the only one who had scored for the Broncos, adding his other two points on free throws. The Broncos battled back to get within two at 16-14 after Austin Swift scored on a layup with eleven minutes, fifteen seconds to play. Lewis hit a jumper to put the Oilers on top 18-14 before the Broncos tied the game at 18-18 with seven minutes and forty seconds left after Walter Thompson hit his second straight jump shot. Parker broke the tie as he converted a turnover into a layup with six minutes, twelve seconds left and Bostic gave the Oilers a 21-18 lead after splitting two free throws. A putback by Roberts off a missed shot and a 3-pointer by Hyde provided Findlay a huge lift and a 26-18 advantage with one minute, twenty-five seconds to go until halftime. Lewis pushed that lead to 28-18 when he threw down a rim-rocking jam with thirty seconds to go, bringing the Findlay fans to their feet.

The Broncos were colder than a winter night in Ohio. The only points they scored in the final seven minutes, twenty-five seconds of the half were off two free throws by Gordon with twelve seconds left. Findlay played tremendous defense the entire half and took a 32-20 lead into halftime. It looked as if the Oilers had control and if they could start the second half the same way they finished the first, they had a chance to put this game out of reach in a hurry. Dwayne Fells ended the field goal drought for the Broncos with a jumper less than a minute into the second half, cutting the Findlay lead to 30-22. Bostic answered with a 3-pointer and Roberts came through with what appeared to be a dagger play as he nailed a shot in the lane and drew a foul. His free throw was on the mark and the Oilers were up 36-22. The Broncos, the upset specialists of the tournament, refused to wave a white flag.

Gordon scored on a layup, Robert Summers knocked down a 3-pointer, Jahn made a layup and Summers hit a pair of free throws and the Broncos were within five at 36-31. The suddenly cold Oilers were on the verge of a collapse. Gordon scored on another drive to the basket with nine minutes, forty seconds to play, displaying the heart he talked about in his interview with me on Friday. Jahn buried a jumper, moments later, trimming Findlay's advantage to 36-35 and the pressure was on. With eight minutes to play, Cal Poly was taking control. Bostic came up with a rebound off a missed shot and was fouled as he turned that second chance into points with a layup. His free throw swished through as well as the Oilers went back in front 38-35. The lead didn't last. Thompson connected from long distance and the Broncos and Oilers were tied at 38-38.

Thompson's shot capped a 16-2 run for Cal Poly. Hyde answered with a jumper that put Findlay in front 40-38 with six minutes, ten seconds left but a trey by Gordon a minute later gave the Broncos their first lead since the beginning of the game. Cal Poly led 41-40 and the Oilers were going to need to dig deep to survive. Lewis helped take the lead back as he scored off a missed shot. Findlay was up 42-41. Bostic had a chance to extend the lead but missed a jumper and Jahn split two free throws to tie the game at 42-42 with one minute, forty seconds remaining. The Broncos tried to steal the momentum but missed on several 3-point attempts as time ticked off the clock. Neither team could deliver a knockout blow. The Oilers and Broncos were headed to overtime.

The Oilers struck first in overtime as Lewis made a shot to give Findlay a 44-42 lead with 4:40 to go. Gordon knotted the score at 44-44 twenty seconds later. Both teams refused to crack and, as far as championship games go, this one was living up to the hype. Bostic's jumper gave the Oilers a 46-44 lead, with a little under four minutes left. It was the last shot Bostic would make. He fouled out less than a minute later, and with the National Player of the Year out of the game, it didn't look good for Findlay. I'm not sure if anyone thought the Oilers could survive the next three-plus minutes without their best player. Bostic sat on the bench clenching a white towel and hoping for the best. Jahn tied the game at 46-46 as he scored on a layup with three minutes, forty-seven seconds to go and drew a foul twenty seconds later, as he split a pair of free throws to give Cal Poly a 47-46 lead. Roberts helped the Oilers take the lead back as he nailed two free throws. Findlay was on top 48-47 but the razor-thin lead hardly eased the concerns of the fans. Gordon's putback gave the Broncos a 49-48 edge before the Oilers missed out on an opportunity to take the lead back as Hyde shot a rare air ball on a 3-point attempt. Gordon's two free throws, with 2:02 to go, nudged Cal Poly in front 51-48. Roberts drew a crucial charge on Cal Poly's next possession and a jumper by Parker cut the Broncos' advantage to 51-50. At that point, there was only one minute, twenty-seven seconds left on the clock. A Cal Poly turnover proved to be a blessing for the Oilers, who managed to tie the game on a free throw by Evans.

The score was tied at 51-51, with less than a minute on the clock. The stage was set for a dramatic finish. In tight games, winning comes down to making big plays and few players were as good in big-time moments as Parker. He was a two-time state champion and made the type of play that left everyone shaking their head. Parker dribbled into the lane and put up a shot. He drew contact as the shot fell through the net. The crowd roared as Parker pumped his fist after coming through in crunch time to give the Oilers a 53-51 lead. Seconds later, Gordon tied the game. Parker tried to answer but his layup was off the mark. There was a scramble on the floor for the ball and, somehow, in a maddening moment, Roberts managed to get his hands on the ball and didn't let go. Findlay was awarded the ball with 2.4 seconds to play on the alternating possession and would have one chance to avoid double overtime.

Both teams took turns calling a timeout, as myself and everyone else in the arena braced for a thrilling finish. I think everyone in the crowd of 4,885 was standing. I've always said the best form of reality television is sports and this game, being aired in front of a national television audience, was as real as it gets. Parker stood near the corner of the baseline under Findlay's basket. Evans came running across the floor and got the ball from Parker in the corner. Dahir Nasser, who was guarding Lewis, broke away and followed Evans. Evans took two dribbles to his left along the 3-point line with Nasser guarding him as tightly as possible the whole way. One of the Cal Poly players near the top of the 3-point line almost came over to help Nasser out. He hesitated instead and didn't make the move. Evans was running out of time to get off a shot. He quickly rose up and faded away as he released the ball with Nasser draped all over him. The ball sailed through the air in a moment where time seemed to stand still and, the next thing I knew, the ball swished through the net. Cheers erupted through the arena from the Findlay fans, who were now overwhelmed with excitement. Evans raced down to the other end of the floor, his arms stretched out, as if he were flying and his teammates poured off the bench to join in on the celebration. Bostic, who had been sitting on the bench watching it all unfold, was the first to leap off the bench and reach Evans, after sprinting down the floor to catch up to him.

Evans hit the shot that every basketball player dreams of making. Only this wasn't a game of pretend in the driveway, school gym or a park. This was real. The Oilers were national champions, a 56-53 victory in the books and a trophy to validate their remarkable run through their season of a lifetime. I stood up and watched the celebration play out. I was overwhelmed with an intoxicating mixture of feelings. I covered this team through its entire journey and to see the Oilers complete it with a championship was amazing. Evans had missed his other three shot attempts in the game—one of his 3-point attempts was even blocked into the stands; but the last shot was the only one that mattered. It was a storybook ending for Evans. Here was a guy who was a team captain, a senior who spent most of the season coming off the bench after being replaced by Hyde in the starting lineup three games into the season. He handled the move with class and defined the meaning of great teammate. He knew being a role player was best for the team and made the most of it. The final play was designed for him to take the shot and he had no intentions of missing it.

"My mindset was that I was going to get a shot off," said Evans, who made 205 career 3-pointers prior to the title game but will be forever remembered for No. 206. "I pictured it as a catch and shoot but I took a couple of dribbles to get a little separation and let it fly."

When the shot went in and the red light above the basket came on as time expired, Evans went crazy. "As soon as it went in, I blacked out, I guess," Evans said. "I probably looked stupid running down the court. I thought I heard the whistle and I hoped the shot counted. It feels like a dream."

A year earlier, the season ended with a nightmare. Grand Valley had stomped on the Oilers' championship dream. A year later, inside the MassMutual Center on a magical March afternoon, the memories of the Sweet 16 loss to the Lakers were trumped by the thrill of being a champion with a 36-0 record, the most wins by an unbeaten champ in the history of Division II basketball.

"I can't express the feeling we have by winning this game the way we did," Niekamp said. "I am so proud of my team, especially the seniors. They have been in the program since they were freshmen. They have had ups and downs, bumps and bruises, disappointments along the way. I can't describe how happy I am for them. It's an unbelievable feeling."

Niekamp was particularly thrilled for Evans. Replays of the shot were shown on the local newscasts Saturday night in Springfield. ESPN made it one of its top 10 plays of the weekend. It was ranked No. 2 but really should have been No. 1. "That shot was right out of the movie Hoosiers," Niekamp said. "I am thrilled this happened to Tyler. He is a Dana Scholar and has the highest grade point average, 3.76, on the team. He lost his starting position but never hung his head. He kept competing. I am so happy for him."

Evans said he joked around Friday about making the game-winning shot in the title game.

"I was joking with Laflin about how cool it would be to hit a game-winning shot," Evans said. "I never thought I would get the chance, much less have the shot go in."

No one was more thankful for Evans' clutch play than Bostic. When he saw Evans release his shot for the ages, he knew it was money in the bank. "I just thank God we won," Bostic said. "I had total confidence in my teammates. Tyler has been making shots like that all year, actually, his whole career. I knew he would make it."

Bostic, who sat next to Evans in the post-game press conference, took a moment to praise Evans for not only hitting a shot that will be remembered forever, but for the way he handled himself all season. Bostic said he nicknamed Evans 'Heavy.' I asked him to elaborate on the remark. "Look at him," Bostic said, pointing to the muscles in Evans' arms. He's a heavy load. Seriously, it's about his mentality. Not a lot of guys can be captain on the No. 1 team, lose their starting spot and not complain at all. He always practiced hard and played hard. It's hard to break Tyler. He's a heavy guy."

As the Oilers took hold of the trophy, I walked onto the floor to join in on the celebration. I know, as a writer, you're supposed to be objective but in this moment, I couldn't help but be overwhelmed with joy as I watched the Oilers celebrate their accomplishment. Several of the players embraced me in between posing for pictures and cutting down pieces of the net. When it came time for Bostic to cut down a piece of the net, he stood at the top of the ladder, scissors in one hand, a piece of the net in the other and looked up, pointing to the sky with both hands. The spirit of Clanton was with Bostic that day, just as it had been with him throughout the Elite Eight and he was gesturing toward heaven to remember Clanton in the moment. Fans broke out in chants of 'Undefeated' as they watched their beloved team bask in the glow of the spotlight. They traveled more than twelve hours to have a chance to witness history, many of them operating on very few hours of sleep and they took pride in knowing their team was on top of the Division II mountain. The climb to the top had been grueling at times, testing the Oilers mentally and physically.

"It's tough to be No. 1 because everyone wants to take their best shot at you," Niekamp said. "They are all trying to make a name for themselves by knocking you off. "But our guys handled this whole thing the right way. It wasn't easy but we did it."

The win provided a sense of relief for a team that, twenty-four hours earlier, looked as if the toll of contending for a championship was starting to catch up to it, especially after surviving three consecutive tournament games decided by 10 points or less. Interestingly enough, Ernst said the Oilers arrived here in Springfield feeling as if a big burden had already been lifted off their shoulders.

"I told the guys when we got here that we just have to go out and do what we have done all season," Ernst said. "If we play well and it's not good enough, we won't have any regrets. To win it all, especially the way we won it, is incredible. I don't know what else to say. It's a great feeling."

Back in October, the mood of the Oilers was different. Everyone knew the Oilers were good enough to win a championship but keeping the No. 1 ranking all year didn't seem realistic.

"I was thrilled we were No. 1 but I knew what would come with it and the burden we would have to carry," Niekamp said. "We weren't overpowering. We lived by grit and guts all year."

The championship would forever belong to the 2008-09 team but, as Ernst had mentioned to me in past interviews, the Oilers' title run was partly a credit to players from the past, particularly the 2002 team that took Kentucky Wesleyan right down to the wire in Findlay's first ever NCAA tournament appearance. That team instilled the belief that the Findlay basketball program was good enough to compete at the highest level. The 2005 Elite Eight team further cemented the belief.

"The players on the 2002 team deserve so much credit," Ernst said. "They gave us the belief that Findlay could compete in Division II circles around the country. Kentucky Wesleyan was the North Carolina of Division II basketball at the time. We went to their home floor, and according to them, played them tougher than anyone had in five years at their place. After that, we felt like we could win at this level."

Seven years later, the Oilers proved it in a way that will be remembered forever.

52 REFLECTION ON THE JOURNEY

As the team partied inside the hotel with family, friends and fans late Saturday night, Lewis stood on the hotel rooftop with Bostic and a couple of his friends, looking out at the city.

"There was a party at the restaurant in the hotel we stayed at. We had three buses fans, parents, students, teachers, everyone you could think of from Findlay was there," Lewis said. "Josh and I were able to escape the madness. We were both looking off the rooftop over the city of Springfield and we both said 'man, we really went undefeated. That's crazy. We never realized it throughout the season'."

The comment speaks to the focus the Oilers maintained during the journey. If the Oilers had lost focus in even the slightest way, the shot of an undefeated season would have gone out the window. Bostic, like Lewis, wasn't surprised the Oilers won the title. "I'm not surprised by the championship, but I am a little surprised by the undefeated thing," Bostic said, in an interview in the summer of 2014. "That season wasn't just about our senior year. It was a tie-in to our junior year. We only lost one player from the 2007-08 team and, when you mix in all of the talent we still had, it was almost like the title was expected."

The focus the Oilers displayed each night was instrumental to their success; the coaches never letting the players get wrapped up in the hype as the wins added up. "Coach Niekamp and Coach Ernst kept us wearing blinders and focused forward," Lewis said. "We didn't get caught up in the ten in a row, twenty in a row or thirty in a row. We took it one game at a time. We knew on any given night we were the better team, as long as we executed our game plan."

For the Oilers, it went beyond the execution of a game plan. The bond forged between Bostic and Lewis was so vital to the success the Oilers enjoyed. They complemented each other and, while both players were clear-cut stars, they never let ego or hunger for stealing the spotlight get in the way of their ultimate goal. Over the course of four years, Bostic and Lewis became the best of friends and the best teammates. For them to end their time together at Findlay as national champions was something they would always cherish. "It was very satisfying winning the title with Morgan after everything we had gone through to get there," Bostic said. "We are still great friends and I'm glad we had a chance to play together and help leave our mark on Findlay basketball."

Lewis appreciated the journey as well and there are no words from him to truly describe what it meant to play alongside Bostic on the road to a championship. "It was special," Lewis said. "To look back and appreciate everything we went through to get to that place, it was a journey I am thankful for. We went through a lot personally, on and off the court. My father passed away, Josh's best friend and grandmother passed away but we were always there for each other. We became family."

The brotherhood extended to the rest of the team as well. Bostic and Lewis never acted as if they were above anyone else. They were class act superstars and never hesitated to give credit to their teammates. It helped forge a tightness among the Oilers that could not be broken.

"All of us on that team have a special brotherhood that is unique in its own way," Lewis said. "The 2009 Findlay Oilers team is a family. It's a true basketball Cinderella story with how everything unfolded. Josh deserved to be player of the year, coach Niekamp deserved the national championship after a legendary coaching career and Tyler Evans deserved to hit that shot. Tyler is one of the most stand-up men I have ever met. There were so many things that made the team special. I'm just blessed God gave me an opportunity to experience a fulfilling four years at Findlay."

EPILOGUE

No team goes into a season thinking it's going to be perfect but from the get-go, the stage was set for a special season. Veteran talent, great role players, a coaching staff that got the best out of its team and, of course, a little luck along the way, all mixed together well to create, as Hyde called it, "a perfect storm".

It's rare to get a perfect storm in sports and the Oilers were recognized for their remarkable accomplishment in May of 2013, when they were inducted into the Ohio Basketball Hall of Fame. Niekamp never imagined he would ever be a coach who was a part of something so special. He only planned to coach for a short period of time before moving on to a new career. As it was, Niekamp stuck with coaching and the rest is history.

"I only planned to coach for ten years and then I was going to get into high school administration," Niekamp said, during an interview a few weeks before the induction ceremony in Columbus. "But new challenges and new goals came up, so I stay motivated to do more."

There were plenty of difficult moments along the way, tough losses to bounce back from, but there were also moments worth savoring. None, however, could top the thrill of coaching a team through an undefeated championship season, all while it held on to the No. 1 ranking. "To be No. 1 in the country all year and go 36-0 and win a national championship is such a great accomplishment," Niekamp said. "It was such a rare thing for any team to do and to be able to win it the way we did makes the title even more special."

Niekamp called the induction into the hall of fame a humbling experience. His players did the same when they took time to reflect on the hall of fame honor and the season they were a part of. Evans, who put the exclamation point on the incredible season with his 3-point shot for the ages, a shot that is still replayed over and over again on the video scoreboard every March at the Elite Eight, told me he was thankful the Oilers were recognized by the hall of fame, and the championship is something he will never forget.

"As far as the hall of fame, it's really not something that I ever considered, but it's definitely something that I'll be extremely proud of for the rest of my life," Evans said in an interview in May of 2013. "I just feel incredibly thankful that I was able to be a part of that team and the UF program. We had a lot of good players on our team, some of them were extremely good, and we had a great coaching staff, but every year there are a lot of teams that can say that. Each year, in every division, there are great teams. The beauty of March Madness is that only one team can be on top, and each year there is a new champion's story. I'm just grateful that my name will always be a part of the championship story from 2009."

Hyde offered an interesting perspective on the season as well prior to the induction. "I definitely appreciate not only the championship but the undefeated season even more now than I did back then. I think it speaks volumes to our mental and physical toughness, our work ethic, desire to win, or more like our hate of losing, and our unselfishness. That was the most unselfish team I have ever played on. There is no way we win the title, let alone go undefeated, if we, collectively, weren't willing to play defense the whole game, dive on the floor, share the ball and out-work every team we played that season."

Niekamp echoed those thoughts and said often that while the Oilers weren't necessarily a perfect team, they were consistent, and ultimately, that was enough. "A team, by definition, makes up for each other's weaknesses, and our guys were able to do that, from the starters to the players we had coming off the bench," Niekamp said. "Everyone played a role. Nothing came easy that season, especially in the tournament, but we found a way to get the job done."

Ernst said the Oilers had a commitment to winning. The humbling loss to the Lakers only strengthened that drive to win. "That group was very special from the moment we started putting it together, particularly the senior class," Ernst said. "I think the year before, when we lost three times to Grand Valley, it kept us humble and hungry for more. Those guys were committed to winning every game that next season. A lot of teams played very well against us, and we still found a way to win."

More than five years later, the final score of every game isn't remembered, but the 36-0 record will never be forgotten. Bostic often uses that unbeaten season as a bragging right with teammates he has played with during his professional hoops career, including many who played at the NCAA Division I level. Being a former Division II player isn't nearly as noteworthy or glamorous, but no one could ever tell Bostic that being a part of an unbeaten championship team wasn't impressive.

"I talk a lot with my teammates about their college careers, and most of them played at big-time schools, but the one thing that keeps little old Findlay in the discussion is that we went 36-0 and won a title," Bostic said in 2014. "It's a feat that even players from top Division I schools must tip their hat to. It makes me proud to say I wore the orange and black. I was blessed to be a part of something special."

It was indeed special, and the more years that go by, the more I realize how truly blessed I was to be the one who chronicled the season of a lifetime. One of my most vivid memories took place after the championship game. I had finished doing interviews and was ready to walk out of the gym with a much different feeling than the one I walked out with a year earlier at Grand Valley. As I headed out of the media room and through the hallway, I saw Lewis. We walked across the gym floor toward the exit. The lights in the gym had been dimmed and arena workers were busy picking up trash around the seats. The giant scoreboard had been lowered to the floor and several people were getting ready to take apart the gym floor. As Lewis and I made our way across the gym, he looked up and saw the banner hanging from the rafters next to the Findlay banners of past D-II champions. He told me a lot of hard work had gone into the banner and he was right. It was an extra special accomplishment for Lewis, who like Bostic, had overcome a great deal to get to this point.

For a moment, I thought back to that March night in Allendale in 2008, arguably the most devastating night in program history. Now, more than a year later, that banner, high above the arena floor, symbolized the Oilers rise from the ashes and the final statement on a perfect run as the No. 1 team in the country.

ABOUT THE AUTHOR

Brian Lester and has a been a sports writer since 1997 and his work has appeared in newspapers and magazines as well as on various sports websites. A native of Rockford, Ill. and an award-winning writer, he began his journalism career by slipping a column on the 1994 NHL lockout under the door of the student newspaper at Rock Valley College. He went on to write for the student newspaper at Eastern Illinois University, where he received a BA in Journalism.

His vast experience as a writer includes work for papers in several states, including a 12-year run covering University of Findlay athletics for The Courier in Findlay, Ohio. He currently works as a sports writer covering high school athletics as well as minor league baseball and college athletics in Florida.

He has a wide range of experience as a freelance writer, doing work for USA Hockey Magazine, D3football.com, D3hoops.com, MiLB.com as well as having articles appear in newspapers such as the Los Angeles Times, Cleveland Plain Dealer and the New York Daily News.

Brian lives in Northwest Florida with his girlfriend and his daughter, who once fell asleep at the press table while coloring during a basketball game, lives in Ohio.

PERFECT RUN AS NO. 1

www.ingramcontent.com/pod-product-compliance
Lightning Source LLC
LaVergne TN
LVHW011345080426
835511LV00005B/136